Praise for

"A rare gem. This book speaks right to the heart and soul of peace and wisdom. Highly recommended reading for everyone."

Richard Carlson, Ph.D
Author of the #1 Bestseller *Don't Sweat the Small Stuff*

"Because a number of books, including my own, have now been written about these three amazing principles, when I read new writing about them I look for heart—I found so much heart in this beautiful little book. I loved it! I'm sure you will too. Thank you, Elsie, for writing it for all of us."

Jack Pransky, Ph.D
Author

"Elsie puts words to everyday situations and observations that clearly show the Three Principles. Her stories gently encourage you to take an honest look at your understanding of what she points to, and in doing so, you are lovingly guided to the quiet space within us for insight to occur. Thank you, Elsie. Practical, yet deeply profound."

Terrie Sanders, BPE, Dip Ed, OAM

Director, Health Pro Consultants Pty Ltd.
Corporate Health Consultant & Gold Medal Paralympian
Recipient, Order of Australia medal.

"I have read the chapters from *Wisdom For Life* many times and each time I have a new insight. The stories and real life experiences shared by Elsie are powerful examples of how change can be so simple, yet so profound, for an individual. Anyone who is on a journey of discovering how they can live a healthy and productive life will gain immense benefit from deepening their understanding of the Principles through Elsie's wisdom."

Gillian Chater
Director, Sagacity Corporation
New Zealand

"Wisdom is not expressed in words, it only reveals itself in the day-to-day living of life. This book provides some great guidance for all of us on the journey of realizing 'The Wisdom Within.' Elsie offers a great collection of stories and examples of how insight unfolds into a wiser navigation through the everyday business of life."

Tim Foley
Human Resources Executive
International Truck and Engine Corporation

Wisdom for Life

Three Principles for Well-being

Elsie Spittle

Lone Pine Publishing

The Publisher and Distributor: Lone Pine Publishing

1808 B Street NW, Suite 140   10145 – 81 Avenue
Auburn, WA, 98001   Edmonton, AB T6E 1W9
USA   Canada

Website: www.lonepinepublishing.com

Library and Archives Canada Cataloguing in Publication

Spittle, Elsie
    Wisdom for life : three principles for well-being / Elsie Spittle.

    ISBN-13: 978-1-55105-510-7
    ISBN-10: 1-55105-510-4

    1. Self-actualization (Psychology) I. Title.

BF637.S4S686 2005   158.1   C2005-904432-2

Editorial Director: Nancy Foulds
Project Editor: Gary Whyte
Production Manager: Gene Longson
Book Design and Layout: Trina Koscielnuk
Cover Design: Gerry Dotto
Scanning, Separations & Film: Elite Lithographers Co.

We acknowledge the financial support of the Government of Canada
through the Book Publishing Industry Development Program (BPIDP) for
our publishing activities.

PC: P5

Table Of Contents

Acknowledgments

Words cannot express my deepest appreciation to Sydney Banks, philosopher and author, for sharing his discovery of the Three Principles. His pioneering, unassuming spirit and unwavering dedication, despite all odds, has continued to inspire and motivate me through the years. Without his work to lead the way, this book and the stories in it would not have been possible.

My heartfelt thanks to my husband, Ken, who has stood by my side these many years. His steadfast love and support has been and continues to be a blessing for which I am exceeding grateful.

Preface

This book is a collection of stories based on my personal insights, experiences and observations. Embedded in these true, heartfelt stories are nuggets of wisdom pertaining to everyday life. My hope is that the power of the principles underlying the human experience, illustrated in the following examples, will help you gain helpful insight into your own life, and in so doing, transform your reality and perhaps touch the world.

Elsie Spittle

Introduction

This book is based on simple principles that have led to a fundamental change in our understanding of how the human experience is created. In 1973, philosopher and author, Sydney Banks, discovered three universal principles—Mind, Consciousness and Thought. Mr. Banks had a profound insight into the spiritual nature of human reality. He told my husband and me that his insight would change the fields of psychology and psychiatry. We felt this was a most unusual statement to make, as Syd has no formal education beyond the 9th grade (age 14) in Scotland so we wondered how he could make such a declaration.

Nonetheless, Mr. Banks' insightful contribution has begun to revolutionize the mental health field, as well as having an impact in the corporate arena, education and medicine. Programs based on the three principles have been established at West Virginia University Medical School as well as at other universities and many private institutions, clinics and organizations.

Over the past 30 years I have seen people from all walks of life who have heard the message of the three principles experience hope and transformation, and I have witnessed what could be called miraculous results. Inner city communities that were filled with despair and desperation have achieved international recognition for their successes in turning around crime-ridden, disadvantaged and seemingly hopeless neighborhoods.

In Santa Clara County in California, principle-based training has resulted in the formation of an entire division within the county dedicated exclusively to the three principles as a helping model. Training is being provided to men and women in the jails and has recently expanded to serve incarcerated juveniles. Drug and alcohol treatment centers have helped people kick their chemical dependency and move beyond recovery into "recovered."

A drop-in center on skid row in Los Angeles found a new way of working with the homeless that allowed people to rediscover their dignity and to cherish their human spirit, which helped them to become productive citizens. One man, in and out of prison on drug charges for most of his life, had this to say. "I got unconditional love there [the drop-in center]. They gave me some hope and self-esteem." He lives in a recovery house now, is working and credits the center with restoring his sense of humanity.

Mental health clinics are offering renewed hope and optimism to their clients in their counseling and therapy. Families and couples that were dysfunctional are finding new satisfaction in their relationships, gently and without having to be traumatized by going into the past to "fix" things. Physicians are working with the mind-body connection, using the three principles to explore deeper levels of sustainable health.

Educators are reaching their students with love and understanding, cultivating an environment where their students are becoming wise and knowledgeable, able to withstand the pressures of modern day life. Corporations are creating a "healthy, high performance" work culture that is producing wiser leaders and happier, more productive employees. Ordinary people who are learning about the principles are discovering new satisfaction, contentment and joy in life.

The principles of Mind, Consciousness and Thought represent the dynamic process, moment-to-moment, by which people generate and know their life experience. These spiritual principles are the answer to why people think, feel and behave the way they do.

They are the answer to heaven and hell here on earth. The realization of these principles is transforming and is the unifying instrument that gives us the power to create our own reality every moment of every day. They are a divine gift.

The principle of Mind is universal creative energy. Consciousness is the ability to be aware of this power and to understand how experience is created. Thought is the capacity to draw on this energy in order to create our experience of reality. We can use this power to create a vast spectrum of experiences, from joy to depression, from contentment to discontent, and from faith to fear. The choice is ours and does not depend on external circumstances.

Those who base their work on these principles have observed that as people begin to realize the operation of these principles for themselves, they gain insights about how to access their own wisdom and common sense. They find calm, clarity, security and a positive direction, regardless of life circumstances, because they see the inside-out nature of experience.

Understanding how our inner wisdom emerges allows us to enhance the qualities of thinking, problem solving and decision making in our day-to-day lives without having to struggle with our past perceptions. It is a natural wisdom that is innate in each and every individual. This inside-out source of resiliency unfolds via a process of insight rather than intellectual learning. As wisdom unfolds it enhances and works in partnership with the intellect, helping people attain a happier, more self-reliant, stable life.

What is so fascinating is that the same set of principles work in every field. Imagine the cost-effectiveness of understanding these principles, in terms of time, energy and financial resources. Consider that you become your own teacher using your own common sense and wisdom. Imagine a world where confidence, stability and a sense of well-being are yours for the making.

Another fascinating aspect is that these principles are a part of each individual, no matter what age, gender, culture, socio-economic background or level of education. The principles work the same way in everyone. If you reflect on this for a moment, you will see that this fact puts all of humanity at the same level and brings about common ground and a measure of equality from which people can treat each other with dignity and respect.

When people hear the word principles they often take it to mean values or personal principles. In the context of this book, I am referring to principles as fundamental forces that are inherent within everyone. These powerful, natural forces give us the capacity to create our personal world.

There is an elegant simplicity to the principles that resonates within people. This resonance uncovers one's own wisdom, leading to insights that act as guides to a more contented life. This resonance is where true, permanent change occurs. This resonance is wisdom in action. Deep inside, everyone already knows what the principles are. We are the principles!

The Mystery of Mind

At first it felt presumptuous to think I could write anything about Mind, but if I was comfortable sharing my understanding of the principles of Consciousness and Thought, why wasn't I comfortable sharing my perspective on the principle of Mind? I realized that I still had beliefs about the omnipotence of Mind and that this particular principle was the most "spiritual" and could not be talked about. Yet aren't Consciousness and Thought "spiritual"?

In this book, spiritual means "intangible," "formless universal energy," "unknown." Webster's dictionary defines spiritual as "of the spirit or soul as distinguished from the body or material matters." These descriptions readily apply to the principles of Mind, Consciousness and Thought.

"Mind, Consciousness, and Thought are all One, called by different names" (*Beyond the Word,* audiotape by Sydney Banks, Minneapolis talk, 1995). This statement clearly delineates the partnership, the same formless energy that comprises all the principles. Does this make it understandable? No. At least not for me. But it's not important to understand the principles intellectually. Actually, it's impossible to understand them intellectually. We struggle so hard with the tangible that we forget about the intangible.

So for me, Mind remains a wonderful mystery. I know that Universal Mind is more than the brain. Mind is spiritual—the brain is physical. I accept the mystery of Mind because I see the results of the principles in action. I know that the more conscious we become of the principles in action, the wiser choices we make in how we use these spiritual gifts. To me this is Wisdom for Life.

The Role of Consciousness

For a long time I thought Consciousness was the ability to bring our thinking to life, via our five senses. Although that made sense to me, I also felt there was something more to Consciousness, something that I was missing. Then it occurred to me that *all* the principles, not just Consciousness, bring our thinking to life. With this I became more aware of the indivisibility of the principles. Yet each principle plays a unique role in providing us with the ability to create our individual experiences. This demonstrates the mystery and the profoundness of the principles. They cannot be understood intellectually and the more we try, the farther away we get. It is a marvelous game.

We can only see or feel the principles in action when we're quiet and still in our personal thinking. When we're gripped by our personal thinking, we often think that we're not using the principles. But that's not true. We're still using the principles but we're using them in a less than healthy manner. We can't get away from using the principles because we *are* the principles.

What was very helpful to me was seeing that Consciousness is awareness *of* and *how* we create experience. That opened a new door of understanding for me. Being aware of experience on an external level is helpful, but being aware of *how* we create experience is the true gift. Here is where free will comes into play, giving us the opportunity to make choices. The gift of Consciousness, being more aware of how we create experience, allows us to make better choices.

There was a time in my life when I was not aware of my experience. I was in denial of much of what I was experiencing. I pretended everything was fine, when in reality, inside me, I was miserable and didn't know how to change my life or myself. It was somewhat helpful when I began to be more aware of what I was feeling but I still didn't know what to do about it. Then I had an insight about how it was my thinking that was creating my feelings. I became conscious of the principles in action. *My ability to think created my reality; my ability to be conscious of that process allowed me to change my reality.*

I heard Syd Banks talk about pure Consciousness being our soul and that touched something deep inside of me. I resonated with that statement. It made more sense to me that if pure Consciousness is our soul, and pure Consciousness is directly connected to and part of universal intelligence, Mind, where all knowledge lies, then the deeper awareness we have of Consciousness, the more we understand life.

The Power of Thought

As people learn about the power of Thought to create our moment-to-moment reality, they sometimes get caught in thinking they need to "reframe, rethink, redirect, re-examine" their thinking. The understanding that all we need is to simply realize *that* we think, and not worry about *what* we think, seems to elude the intellect. Yet this understanding is where we gain the freedom from the stress of analyzing the myriad thoughts that we are thinking. What a marvelous gift this understanding is to humanity. Imagine the energy that people would have if they didn't have to examine their thinking, didn't have to be concerned about *where* that particular thought came from and *why* they are thinking it!

It is this type of overly analytical personal thinking that erects a barrier to our innate wisdom. The more we realize this, the more we live in a world of insights which come from the universal intelligence that we are all part of and connected to. Our lives become so much simpler and we find time to enjoy what life has to offer. Even when stressful things come up, our trust in and reliance on our innate wisdom provides the answers to our problems.

The best way to recognize when we are engaged in our personal thinking is by the feeling we are experiencing. If the feeling is a negative feeling, i.e., worry, mistrust, skepticism, resentment, doubt, then we are using our thinking against ourselves. Simply recognizing this feeling and realizing that the feeling comes from thought will defuse the intensity, and unless we continue to entertain our personal thinking, the feeling will vanish.

We are always thinking, but there is a different quality of thought when we are not erecting barriers to our innate wisdom. Insightful thoughts fill the space left by all the negative, worrisome thoughts we used to entertain so much. These new thoughts are calming, inspiring, exhilarating, and exceedingly helpful. These thoughts guide us to a better life.

The feelings of gratitude and deep appreciation for what we are finding is the route to contentment and Wisdom for Life.

The Power of Hope

I had the privilege to visit a residential alcohol and drug recovery home for women. One of the treatment programs at the lodge is based on the principles of Mind, Consciousness and Thought. Seeing this treatment program in action was a powerful, inspiring, hopeful experience for me. It provided an opportunity to gain a fresh and deeper appreciation for the power of hope that the principles offer to people from all walks of life, in this instance for people struggling with substance addictions.

The first thing that struck me when I walked in and met the counselors and the group of women was the feeling of warmth and caring that was present, a very comfortable and safe environment. After I was introduced and was able to share a bit of my story, I invited the women to share their stories with me, letting them know that I wanted to be able to pass their stories on to people in other countries that I would soon be visiting. The women poured their hearts out, expressing their deep gratitude for what they were discovering within themselves. These are some of their comments:

1. *"I've gained an appreciation of my own wisdom and common sense. When I first arrived here, I would ask my counselor for answers to my problems. She wouldn't tell me what to do; instead she pointed me to my own wisdom*

and told me that I had the answers inside. At first I couldn't believe it, that she wouldn't help me, because in other programs that's what the counselors did, they tried to 'fix' us. Then I had an insight about my problem and I realized the counselor was right—I did have the answers inside! Now I know that all I have to do is get quiet in my thinking, and the solutions will come."

2. *"I always thought I was damaged goods and that there was no hope for me. When the counselors told me I had innate health, I didn't know what they meant. Nobody had ever told me that before. Now I feel better about myself and feel like I have a future. I no longer have to delve into my past to find happiness. All that really matters is what's happening right here, right now, and what I think of myself. Not what others think of me."*

3. *"Other traditional programs focus on the 'disease' of addictions, and that I would always be an alcoholic. I used to feel so bad that when I got out, I drank even more to deaden the pain. This is the first one that focused on 'health.' I felt such relief at hearing this. I didn't have to label myself any longer. It helped me realize that the principles that I used to create my addiction could be used to create a healthy life, free of my addiction."*

4. *"I learned about the principles while I was in jail, then I came to the recovery center to continue my treatment. I learned to trust that my children also had innate health and that they will be OK. That gave me such hope and relief, and has deepened our relationship. I always felt so*

bad that I couldn't care for them while I was in jail and didn't know that they had resilience within them to help them while I was incarcerated. This has helped my recovery process so much."

5. *"We get a chance to rest and reflect while in treatment. I was exhausted and felt hopeless when I arrived. I've been on the streets for 15 years, just struggling to survive and to support my habit. I've never had the opportunity to rest and reflect in a safe place before. Other programs I've attended have kept us busy 24–7, filling us with information and never giving us a moment to ourselves. The counselors here trust us and help us to learn to trust ourselves."*

6. *"Over the past 13 years, I have been very involved in a traditional treatment program. Although I had over five years clean and sober at one time, I have not been able to maintain my sobriety. Since being introduced to the principles I have gotten a much deeper understanding of myself, and the way my 'conditioned' thinking has affected me in the past. I now see how my thoughts create my own reality, and the endless possibilities for a happier, healthier future."*

7. *"When I learned about the principles, it touched my soul. It gave me back my power. I always knew something was missing but I didn't know what. Now I do and it's changed my life."*

I hope these comments give others who are struggling with addictions some hope and inspiration. We have an incredible resource in understanding the principles, as we wait for the addictions field to notice a new, health-oriented approach. I applaud the pioneers who are sharing this understanding with others in this field and I have the deepest respect and admiration for those in recovery who have the courage to see beyond the labels innocently applied to them by themselves and by society, and who say proudly, "I am recovered!"

* * *

I was invited to conduct a public seminar in Basel, Switzerland. Basel is a beautiful city on the banks of the Rhine River, with the magnificent 12th-century Münster Cathedral located in the heart of the city, near the bustling *Marktplatz* (Market Place).

Before I started the program, I had wondered about the different languages and how that would affect my communication and rapport with the group. Most of the audience were Swiss and German and were fairly fluent in understanding English. Still, I felt there would be certain words and phrases that I was counting on my colleague, who arranged the seminar, to translate.

Despite stopping the program many times to translate, the connection and understanding flowed between the participants and myself. It amazed and touched me that the language barrier was really nonexistent, except in my head. Stronger than the difference in language was the deep feeling of goodwill. Clearly the principles of human experience resonated with all the participants and brought forth an understanding beyond language.

Early in the program, a young musician told us he felt disillusioned and put off with society because of how careless people are with caring for their environment, for nature, and he felt hopeless seeing how the planet is polluted. He wondered how understanding the principles of Mind, Consciousness and Thought could help the environment. Rather than answering him, I asked him to hold the question until the end of the program and see if the answer would come to him.

His response at the end of the three days was to share his new understanding that when people get in touch with their wisdom, they start to see their surroundings with new eyes and with more respect, and automatically take better care of nature. That is when he said, "I have fallen in love with humanity."

A kindergarten teacher shared an example of going to a beach in Greece while on vacation, and seeing garbage littered on the beach, spoiling the pristine beauty of the white sand and turquoise water. She was compelled to go back to the car for garbage bags and started to pick up garbage. A man who came along and saw her doing this, reached down for a bag and began to help. Shortly, the beach was clean and restored to its original beauty. She told of feeling "so good" to have done this and how pleased she was that her actions had inspired another to help. "How easy it would be to clean up our world if more people were in touch with their wisdom," she said.

Another man spoke of understanding "depth of feeling" for the first time. He said that when he first heard people talk of deepening their understanding of the principles, he didn't know what that meant. He thought of depth as a "hollow hole" and couldn't connect that to the principles. For the first time he felt full of deep feelings inside of himself and understood the significance of "deepening our understanding." He told of going home to his family that evening and seeing them with fresh, appreciative eyes, with more love. When the children got a little rambunctious, it didn't bother him. In his newfound calmness, he enjoyed their energy and soon they quieted down.

Another woman, head of an agency that specializes in working with dyslexic individuals, spoke of rediscovering the "fertile silence" of her youth, saying that she had forgotten the power and benefit of the silence within. She was deeply moved by realizing that this silence was still within her. She related how this helped move her beyond "not understanding the principles." She realized the "feeling" was the most important thing and understanding would come with the feeling. She was beginning to realize that wisdom is beyond the intellect and that when wisdom is uncovered, it is accompanied by a positive, warm feeling of well-being. She became more comfortable that her intellect would "catch up" with wisdom and via insight, would understand more about the principles.

A financial advisor from Geneva voiced his opinion that if key world leaders were able to engage their wisdom, as the participants had in the program, the world would soon be a much better place in which to live. He envisioned the business world working in partnership with communities and countries in need, without thought of territorial boundaries, but seeing and addressing the needs of humanity, together, in harmony.

A professor of social work from Lucerne told a moving story of a woman he was counseling who had a tumor on her brain. She needed an operation but understandably was very nervous about the situation. As the professor calmed her down, he told her a little about her innate health and how that was always present within her to help her in this trying time. Somehow his calming manner and his words seemed to soothe her before she had her operation. She came through in good health.

During my time in Basel, I conducted two programs, one week apart. In the first course, the energy and learning was high, full of the wonder of exploring the depths of the human spirit. In the second program, a week later, the energy was rich, fertile and peaceful in the process of discovery. Insights were abundant, with many practical examples of seeing the principles in action, of using the principles in a healthy manner, rather than "practicing" or "applying" them.

There were long periods of "fertile silence," a contented, comfortable quiet. A psychologist from Germany, who really didn't understand English very well, commented that she had never experienced this spontaneous, natural quiet, where someone hadn't said, "let's be quiet now." Clearly, we were experiencing the power of people gathered together, in alignment and harmony with each other, each contributing their own energy, wisdom and peace.

The Confusion of Simplicity

Often when the principles of Mind, Consciousness, and Thought are introduced to a new audience, some participants will experience an interesting phenomenon. They will talk about their confusion but at the same time will express that they are very engaged in what you are saying. They will say things like, "I don't have a clue what you are talking about, but I can see there is something different in what you are saying and I'd like to learn more." Or they might say, "I still don't understand the principles, but I'm having a lovely time."

When the intellect is introduced to the simplicity of wisdom, the result, usually, is confusion. When the intellect is introduced to complexity, the result is also confusion. The difference between the two kinds of confusion is the *feeling*.

The confusion related to simplicity is usually an engaging feeling, full of curiosity and puzzlement, and is often accompanied by a feeling of warmth and relaxation, almost in spite of ourselves. This is an unusual combination, to experience confusion and yet to enjoy the puzzlement. It takes some understanding to get used to this illogical situation.

The feeling that accompanies the confusion that arises from complexity is a stressful feeling, a feeling of resistance and of trying to "figure it out." This leads to many questions from the participants, and not much listening. This feeling affects other participants and before you know it, as the facilitator, you may feel compelled to try to explain, even further, what the principles are and how they work. Of course this confuses the issue even more.

What I've learned to trust, in this situation, is the *feeling* or *tone* in the room, coming from the participants and coming from me. I can feel the difference between confusion from simplicity and confusion from complexity; too much explanation of what is, essentially, unexplainable; the conundrum of trying to explain the formless into form. The more I realize that such explanations are impossible, and the more I trust that when people's wisdom is engaged, they will *realize* the principles, rather than *figure out* the principles, the deeper into understanding, we, as a group, are able to go.

As a facilitator, the confusion expressed by the participants as a result of my over-explaining the principles used to unnerve me. Consequently, I would redouble my efforts to explain even more, thinking that I was "breaking it down" so people could better understand. This process of "breaking it down" inevitably elicited more questions, thus more explanation.

I began to realize that, naturally, people would be confused, at first, by the principles, because they were being introduced to something that was unfamiliar. When I realized that, it allowed me to relax and not be taken aback by their confusion. Now I help people to get comfortable with their confusion and to see it as a healthy process that leads to understanding. I let people know that I would rather have someone tell me they are confused than have people confidently assure me that they know what I'm talking about and then promptly ask many questions clearly indicating they don't know.

An example is a young woman who attended a program at the request of her supervisor. Her supervisor had previously attended a course and found it very helpful. She wanted her staff to experience the benefits of understanding how we create human experience. I had talked to the group about how the program I would be presenting was a different kind of learning, that the learning in this program was a process of insight, rather than learning via memory. I also mentioned that the pace of learning might feel slow compared to the speed and the volume of information one tends to receive at many seminars. We talked about how, when our personal thinking slows down, insights occur that add to our understanding of the principles.

The young woman was quite confused the first morning and in the afternoon asked when we would be getting to the heart of the program, explaining that she wasn't used to not getting a lot of handouts. "Although I appreciate not having to learn new techniques and find it rather refreshing, I don't feel like I'm learning anything." I asked her if she was enjoying the refreshing feeling of not learning techniques and her response was, "Yes, but I still think that it would be better if you explained the principles more." I asked her to be patient and just let the refreshing feeling carry on and that we would continue to bring the principles into all the topics we discussed.

The next day when she arrived, I was pleased to see that she was looking relaxed. She was quieter that day, had fewer questions and seemed more at ease. After lunch, when we did some small group work, she seemed animated and was joining the laughter coming from her group. At the end of the day, when I had participants share, if they wanted, what they had learned, she spoke of her confusion early in the program, and how difficult it was for her to slow down, given her busy pace of life. She mentioned that she felt relaxed and was enjoying herself, but still felt she hadn't learned anything.

Then she proceeded to tell us about an interaction with her boyfriend the previous evening, and that she hadn't responded in the same old way. It occurred to her that her boyfriend was caught up in his thinking and taking it out on her. She decided she didn't like the feeling of their discussion and was able to instill a sense of calm into the conversation, which then defused the situation. I smiled at her as I said, "And you didn't learn anything in this program, is that right?"

Her face went blank for a moment, and then she lit up like a candle. "I guess I did. It seems so simple, too easy, that I didn't even realize what happened. It just occurred to me that I didn't want to go in that negative direction and so I didn't, and neither did my boyfriend. But he doesn't think this program makes sense, either." Everyone burst out laughing and we agreed that was another topic.

The intellect operates at a slower pace than wisdom, so sometimes it appears as if we've learned nothing, when in reality the insight or "it occurred to me" is so natural that we don't realize what we've learned until after the fact. What I've discovered is that the more we trust and rely on our wisdom, the more our intellect and wisdom come closer in alignment. Then the duality of life becomes One.

Faith – Does it Work?

When people are first introduced to the *inside-out* nature of generating the human experience, a question of faith arises. To understand what *inside* means requires faith and the experience of insight.

Many people view life from the outside-in, believing that events, circumstances and situations are the cause of their problems. I certainly did. I thought that the fact that I had been brought up poor, with a limited education, was the reason for my insecurity. I had no conception that the way I *thought* about those circumstances, those insecure thoughts, created my feelings of insecurity. For 30 years I thought that way, blaming external events and circumstances for my problems, for my apparent inability to get ahead in life. To feel content with life was a pipe dream, as far as I was concerned. I thought you needed material things; success in your work, financial stability and recognition—all these spelled success to me.

When I got a glimmer that my insecure thinking was creating my feelings of insecurity and my insecure behavior, my world was transformed. No longer could I blame external circumstances for my predicament. With understanding came new confidence and faith that life was unfolding with greater wisdom than I was aware of.

I began to see predictability in the principles of human experience, just as there is predictability in the principles of mathematics. Two plus two equals four. This equation is always correct. Two plus three does not make four, only two plus two equals four. Anywhere we go in the world, this equation is the same. Other cultures use the same math; if they add two plus two, they also arrive at the figure four. This principle of calculation provides us with balance and stability.

Carpenters need to understand basic math, otherwise the house they build will be on an uneven and unstable foundation. All physicists, engineers, mechanics and computer technicians use mathematics; the list can go on and on. Likewise, we need to understand how we build our experience of life. This commonality also provides us with balance and stability. Anywhere we go in the world, the principles of human experience work the same way, not only for us, but for everyone. As we think, so we are. There is complete confidence in this, which brings faith.

Faith is often described as "unquestioning belief." Syd Banks describes faith as "knowledge manifested into form." Knowing and beliefs are two different capacities. Knowing comes from inside and beliefs are outside. Beliefs can change; knowing gets deeper. You practice beliefs; you live in faith. "Your wishes will be granted because you start to live in faith" (*Our True Identity*, Sydney Banks audiotape).

Recently, my husband, Ken, and I started our own business. We were partners in a successful enterprise that provided principle-based training programs to a wide variety of communities and organizations. We both were feeling that we wanted to move out on our own but were fearful of making the move. We had financial security with a project funded by a large community grant for the next four years and we had a promising future with other projects in the works.

Yet our wisdom kept knocking on our door, encouraging us to spread our wings and be open to other opportunities. Both of us continued to ignore our wisdom and listen to our personal thinking, which was encouraging us to stick with the known and to stick with the financial security. This was a dilemma that provided us with much angst that caused us to wake up in the middle of the night to ponder.

Finally, during a meeting with our business partner, much to my surprise, words came out of my mouth that started the process of leaving the company. The words had popped out of their own accord, as if driven by something other than myself. However, no sooner were the words spoken than I knew they were right.

When we left the meeting, the feeling of elation filled both of us with gratitude. Fear had turned to faith and we've never looked back. Opportunities for work presented themselves from out of the blue, for which we were exceedingly grateful. We're finding that gratitude nourishes faith and we're finding that faith is nourishing our personal relationship.

Another example of faith comes to mind. A woman who was part of a long-term training program related this story at one of the sessions. She had tried to purchase a house a year before and was told that she didn't earn enough to qualify for the loan. Over the course of the year she learned about the principles and really took them to heart and her life began to change. She was promoted at work, her relationship with her husband and children improved substantially, and she had never felt happier. She applied again to the same place for a low-income loan to purchase the house and was told that she now earned too much! It was recommended that she fudge the details of her dependents and expenses so that she would qualify for the loan. She thought long and hard about this. She really wanted this house. Finally she came to peace that if she was meant to have the house, she would get it, but she could not be out of integrity with her soul. So she told them she couldn't do it. A week later, they called her and told her they had reviewed her application and she was approved for the loan... .

Faith or fear? Does faith work? I leave it to you to decide.

Listening for Wisdom

One of the first things you'll notice when you engage your inner wisdom is that the quality of your listening is enhanced. The quality is enhanced because your personal thinking is quieting down and your mind is clear, open and more sensitive to the nuances behind what is being said.

You are the first to benefit by this change in awareness. You will find yourself tuning in and paying more attention to your inner voice. You will be surprised at the wisdom that occurs to you, things that you've never thought of before. Creativity is unleashed within and you may find yourself doing things you never thought you were capable of doing.

Your ability to listen to others improves. In the helping profession, in communities and organizations, when we were called upon to counsel or coach people, traditionally we would listen for specific issues or problems, assess them, then work together with the client to resolve them. Many years ago, when I was a novice in the helping profession, listening for the issues, then resolving them with the client was considered leading edge. Prior to that, most social workers and human resources personnel were trained to "fix" their clients. Fixing our clients often led to us taking on the problems of our clients, sympathizing with them, judging them, being disappointed in them and so on. This approach led to burnout and, perhaps, to even leaving the profession, let alone taking the burnout home and not being present for our own families, because we were too tired and stressed.

Now that we are enjoying our own wisdom and see that everyone has the capacity to be healthy and wise, we know that we no longer have to "fix" people. Rather, we point people in the direction of their own common sense and they learn through insight how to solve their own problems, how to enjoy and appreciate life more. In essence, they learn to *listen* to their own wisdom.

This depth of understanding and listening does away with burnout. People who are immersed in this type of listening remain energized, creative and wise, knowing what to do in the moment, no matter the situation. A counselor related the following story to me. She was giving a workshop to a group of social workers when one woman, during the session, appeared to become upset and fled from the room. The counselor soon finished her presentation and after talking with a few people, made her way to the back of the room, looking for the participant who had left. She couldn't find her so she went to the ladies room. There in a corner, was the woman who had left, weeping her eyes out. There was no one else in the room. The counselor went to her and asked if she could help. The woman shook her head then proceeded to pour out her distress. The counselor just listened, said nothing, but just listened. The woman quieted down, regained her composure and they both went back to the session.

Later that week the counselor got a call from the woman who thanked her profusely for listening to her. She told her how much this quiet listening had helped, that she hadn't wanted any advice, but someone to just listen, and how healing this had been, calming her down and leading her to her own insights about her situation.

The counselor told me that she really hadn't known what to do when she approached the distressed woman. She didn't know who she was or what was troubling her. What came to her was to do nothing, just to be there for the woman, to be present and listen. She herself was startled at the impact of this quality of listening, saying that it reinforced her own understanding of the power of compassion and an open heart.

A participant in our program, a student working toward his degree in social work, stated he knew what "quiet listening" was. He called it "passive listening." As I listened to him, what finally came to light was that his understanding entailed listening to his client without saying anything until he heard the problem clearly identified, saw the red flag, then could help his client move toward a solution. He truly felt this process was the same thing we were talking about, not realizing that we were listening for wisdom, for common sense, not for problems. Once he *realized* the difference, he was able to listen for the inner health in his clients and point them in the direction of their own wisdom. It is in this wisdom that solutions occurred to them, shedding light on their issues and moving them to peace of mind.

Here's another example. A colleague called me one day, very upset and close to tears. Apparently she had had a falling out with a close friend and couldn't understand why they couldn't hear each other's point of view. She went on for some length about this dilemma. She was familiar with the principles and was very wise but at this moment in time, her personal thinking covered her wisdom. She couldn't get in touch with her wisdom, or so she thought. As I listened to her, beyond her problem, what I heard was her wisdom. The fact that she had reached out and called showed her wisdom. When I pointed this out to her, she paused for a moment. I could *hear* her mind get quiet. Then she said in an awed voice, "That's right, I did call, didn't I? So my wisdom is still there! I just didn't realize it."

Another example comes to mind of the experience of an executive performance coach who shared this story with me. Prior to his introduction to deep listening and innate health, his coaching was based on the traditional approach. He would observe his client in action, give him feedback on what his weaknesses were and what his strengths were, in that order. He would then suggest strategies to his client on how to improve his performance. He would take the time at the beginning of the session to establish rapport with the executive being coached, but often the client became uncomfortable during the feedback session. This discomfort posed a problem for the coach because the client stopped listening. Sometimes the performance of the client improved and sometimes it didn't. It was a hit and miss process.

The coach gained an understanding that people have a natural capacity for innate confidence. He now helps the executives he works with see and gain access to the unplumbed depth of performance inside themselves. His work became more successful, with more hits than misses. Some of his clients were skeptical at first but as they uncovered their deeper level of confidence and saw their performance improve, they spread the word. Now the coach is busier than ever.

Listening for wisdom engages wisdom. Listening for problems engages problems. Listening for wisdom engages insights to solve problems. Listening for problems engages more problems... .

The Heart of Relationships

The heart of relationships is love, unconditional love. This applies to all relationships, personal and professional. We may not call it love in regard to professional relationships. We may call it caring, respect or rapport, but nonetheless, at the heart, at the core of the relationship, love is the enhancer.

How do we achieve the state of unconditional, neutral love? By understanding that the principles of Mind, Consciousness and Thought create the human experience. By understanding that we all have innate wisdom and innate health residing deep within our consciousness. When we see that we are all the same inside, this knowledge somehow lends itself to feelings of greater caring.

For the purpose of this story, I will focus on innate health and tie it back to the principles. Many people don't recognize the gift of innate health; people don't know that everyone is born with wisdom, just as we are born with the principles active within us. The nature of life is such that as we become conditioned by society, culture, upbringing, education and the influence of our peers, we lose sight of the light within us. When we regain the understanding that we are inherently healthy, we gain a new benchmark from which to view ourselves, as well as the rest of the world.

This understanding provides a fresh perspective, allowing us to see beyond behavior to the inner core of health in individuals, thus reducing judgment and promoting compassion, enhancing all relationships. Even when others aren't aware of the gift of innate health, but you are, there will be a greater understanding that will provide a buffer in difficult situations.

Another benefit of innate health is the ability to take things less personally. Understanding that people aren't "out to get you" but are doing the best they can, given their level of understanding, provides a wonderful feeling of freedom. It allows you to see beyond their words and actions to see their psychological innocence.

For example, once I became mentally healthier, my treatment of my husband and children improved considerably. I became less judgmental, less critical, took things less personally and became more loving and patient. My love was more unconditional. My love didn't depend on my family living up to my high expectations. I was more inclined to accept them for who they were at that moment, not who I wanted them to be. I didn't react with anger when they did things that I used to think were deliberate, because I understood they were doing what made sense to them, given their state of mind at that moment. This realization relieved an enormous amount of stress in our family.

In turn, our family members became healthier, as they accessed their wisdom, yet they often did not even realize this was happening. The process of engaging another's health is such a natural outcome of your contented state of mind that you aren't necessarily aware that it's happening, and yet you feel the benefits of this outcome by the improvement in your relationships.

A situation occurred with my daughter when she was 12 years old. She was struggling with adolescence and was not very happy, moping in her room, refusing to clean it, getting poor marks in school and, in general, trying my patience. At first I was able to see her unhappiness with compassion but after awhile my compassion was replaced with frustration. I tried talking with her about her unhappiness, to respect her state of mind but also to make light of it, hoping I could tease her out of it, so she wouldn't continue to take things so seriously. That didn't work.

The situation worsened. She became even more morose, her room dirtier and she started to skip school. My frustration turned to anger and understanding completely disappeared. I grounded her for life… .

Then a close friend who was aware of the situation suggested I clean her room for her and take her out for a nice lunch and a movie or whatever she wanted to do, but to spend some loving time with her. Well, at first this idea went absolutely against the grain! Clean her room? Take her to lunch? When she was skipping school? This was asking too much.

But when I calmed down and my wisdom emerged, it made sense to me. I could see that my daughter wanted to be happy but didn't know how at that point in her life. When my focus was on what was wrong with her, that is what I experienced. The principles in action brought to life my thoughts about what was wrong with my daughter—that she was sloppy, that she didn't care about her school work, and so on. When my focus shifted and I saw her core of health again, my heart went out to her and I was able to appreciate her and express my unconditional love. Now, the principles brought my positive thoughts to life—that my daughter was doing the best she could and that she was a loving, caring individual.

I did clean her room and enjoyed it. We went to lunch and shopped for a new desk for her room. We had a good time together and there was a definite shift in our relationship. It wasn't all peaches and cream after that but we both learned to *listen* to each other with more depth, without our personal thinking getting in the way so much of the time.

The benefits of seeing innate health affects work relationships as well. Much of the success of our work in communities and organizations is because of the level of rapport we are able to achieve with people—particularly with people who are stressed and feeling hopeless. Initially they may resist, but when their behavior fails to elicit judgment from us, and instead elicits compassion, their health is engaged and hope appears. As they begin to realize their own wisdom, they spread it to others, and the ripple effect is in motion.

Communication improves because people listen better; cooperation is enhanced because there is less competition. When you are operating from a healthy state of mind, you automatically listen at a deeper level. When you feel good about yourself, there is no need to prove yourself competitively. Rather you are inclined to work together, ensuring the best effort will be achieved.

I've seen the same thing in communities. When residents in a core group start to access their inner wisdom and their lives are transformed, their neighbors wonder what is happening. They become curious and are drawn to the nice feeling that people are experiencing. Soon they too become aware of their own wisdom.

The process of building rapport and positive feelings is how families, communities and organizations are transformed. Simply by realizing our innate health and that we are the principles in action, a natural process is unleashed and change occurs. Not everyone in the family, community or organization will change, but they will be touched. Then it is up to individuals to travel their road.

The Perfection of Imperfection

One of the most helpful things I have learned in my journey is not to take life and personal growth so seriously. Once I began to see that human experience is created from the inside-out, I became a serious student, learning more about the principles and how life worked. The more serious I became, the more judgmental I became about others and myself. I could see clearly how people created drama in their life and didn't hesitate to point out, lovingly, I thought, how it was their thinking that created the drama. Needless to say, this criticism didn't always endear me to my family or friends.

I was very hard on myself, feeling guilty if I thought negative thoughts, berating myself that I *should* know better, then feeling worse instead of better. Then I realized that feeling worse was not the direction to go to find well-being. This insight brought humor, understanding and great relief to the situation, allowing me to be gentler and more accepting of my own and other's imperfections. I realized that both perfection and imperfection are the principles in motion. The first step toward perfection is accepting your imperfections and learning from them, knowing that this life is an infinite journey.

Recently a young counselor who was relatively new to the understanding of how experience is created called me with a question about her work. Her boss had given her an opportunity to do a seminar based on the principles and she was feeling anxious. She said, "I don't feel worthy of this opportunity to train others when I don't live in a mentally healthy state all the time. What can I possibly teach others?"

Her earnest question engaged my heart and I heard her humility and also her genuine distress. As we chatted I asked her what she had found most meaningful about her new understanding. She reflected for a moment then said, "The fact that we think and have a choice about what we think is remarkable to me."

"Do you feel that would be helpful for others to know?" I asked.

"Why of course," she replied.

"What else did you find most helpful?" I asked her.

"Knowing that my feelings are a directional guide to mental health," she said. "Feelings are like the compass consistently pointing to the north. We have our own internal compass, unerringly pointing us to our true north—well-being."

"How do you feel now?" I enquired.

"Great," she responded. "I just *heard* myself and realized what I was doing with my own thinking! Thank you so much for all your help."

I chuckled as I pointed out that she really had helped herself but I appreciated her gratitude.

Here's another example of the perfection of imperfection. A community revitalization project where I've been conducting a training program experienced a traumatic event. The housing manager related this story during one of the training sessions.

The community is a new housing complex that replaced old, dilapidated apartments. The housing manager and the residents are very proud of their new community and the residents, for the most part, have taken good care of their homes. Recently a fatal shooting occurred that shocked the whole neighborhood. The housing manager was understandably distressed and felt betrayed by this action, feeling that she had treated the residents so well and yet here was this terrible thing happening.

The housing manager immediately called upon the staff of the community project. All the staff and the housing manager are part of the training program. The staff showed much wisdom, understanding and respect for what the residents were going through and this helped defuse the situation. They brought 60 to 70 people together, helped calm them down, and elicited the residents' wisdom and creativity about how to help the community and residents become safer and more responsible for each other, rather than just for their own families and children. They came up with ideas such as phone lists for each other, how to contact each other quickly, how to supervise other children when their parents weren't home, and so on.

The housing manager, who had been gripped by her personal thinking, was able to disengage from her feelings of betrayal and distrust. Once she let those thoughts and feelings go, her wisdom emerged and she began to work with the residents and project staff to come up with meaningful, peaceful solutions.

What was a tragedy ended up bringing the community together, working in harmony, rather than advocating for peace with more contention and violence. One participant pointed out that sometimes tragedy leads to empowerment and something meaningful can be the result. This tragedy, imperfection certainly, was a step toward perfection and the empowerment of individuals and the community as a whole.

Hungry for Wisdom

In the aftermath of the horrendous, heartrending tragedy that struck America on September 11, 2001, I had no words of wisdom to offer. I, like the rest of America and much of the world, was grief stricken and heartsick at what had befallen our nation. Nonetheless, my soul offered solace and I knew that many individuals' own wisdom would rise to meet their needs, if they wanted it and if they allowed it to emerge.

What I would like to offer are some observations. My husband Ken and I watched a special edition of a television program a few nights after the event. The moderator interviewed six young university students, all with different ethnic backgrounds. One was a Mexican American, two were African American, one an Arab American and two were Caucasian. One of the African Americans said, "Please take off the prefix before American. We are all American. We need to unite and go beyond ethnicity." Another of the students said, "You can't meet anger with anger, nor violence with violence. You will only get more anger and violence."

I was struck by the wisdom of these young people, our future leaders, and frankly our leaders now. Ken was also struck by this and pondered, "What if the government leaders said, we won't retaliate. Let's resolve this peacefully. What would happen?"

Sounds far fetched, I know. But it seems to me the world is hungry for wisdom, indeed, crying out for wisdom. Perhaps this tragedy can illuminate an internal path toward our soul, where all wisdom and solutions reside. We *are* hungry for wisdom and are astonished when we realize it is hidden in what appears to be the least likely but most accessible spot—within our own psyche.

Recently we conducted three seminars in three different countries in Europe. All the people were of different cultures, had different beliefs, spoke different languages. All had one thing in common. They have the ability to create their experience of life via Mind, Consciousness and Thought, whether they realize it or not. When they were pointed to their birthright and connected to their own wisdom, the feeling of wonder and lightheartedness filled them to the brim. Solutions to questions and problems came to them through the mystery of insight, the bubbling up of wisdom just waiting to be unleashed.

We conducted one program for a group in which initially there were several who were doubtful that there is such a thing as universal wisdom. Many of these people had strong beliefs that wisdom is subjective. At one level, it is true, wisdom is subjective. But when the intellect is stilled for a moment, universal wisdom has the opportunity to slip through the filters of our personal thinking and shine a light on our world.

This was a revelation to many at this seminar, and some of the participants resonated with enthusiasm. Others were less enthused though they were thoughtful and confused, which I took as a good sign. Considering the confusion and having conducted some private interviews with a few participants who expressed a desire for more practical information, we decided on the second day to focus the seminar on more work-related issues, still connecting the issues to the principles, but not as deeply as before. As we proceeded, things seemed to settle down and the seminar ended on a nice note with people expressing their gratitude.

Several days later, I had the opportunity to meet with the CEO of the group we had worked with. He had also attended the program. When I asked him what people had gotten from the seminar, this is what he had to say. "The consensus is that they wished you had shared more on the principles and not focused on the work issues. They realized, after they had time to reflect and absorb the new information, that they wanted to learn more about the principles and their wisdom."

I was astounded to say the least. Yet when I heard him, I realized instantly, once again, that when some people are first introduced to this inner understanding there can be a time gap before the intellect catches up with wisdom. That time gap is what creates the initial confusion. When there is time for reflection, there is time for wisdom and the intellect to work in partnership, to be in harmony, to lead us in a better, more fruitful direction.

For me, the lesson was a deepening of my faith, trusting the power of wisdom to work its magic. It was a time for my wisdom and intellect to merge—to see that there is a balance between helping people feel safe and the need to always keep the primary focus on the principles of human experience, to realize that there is a spiritual process at work, before form, and that is the direction to point people. That takes faith, both for the facilitator and for the participants.

Faith is contagious—if you have faith, it prompts and engages others' faith at a deeper level. Faith emerges when you are present in the moment, in communion with universal wisdom. Faith also prompts the neutrality of observation rather than judgment.

Judgment comes from the intellect and brings negative feelings. Observation comes from wisdom and brings compassion.

Let us unite together in faith, harmony and compassion. Surely this will help the world.

The Peace of Reflection

One of the best things we have in life as human beings is an innate ability to move on—past trauma, past suffering or judgment and retaliation. The example of children's resiliency is one to model. That's not to say that we don't hold people accountable for their actions, but it is *how* we do this that counts.

If we can come from a position of understanding that people do what they do because of how they think, we then have wisdom to help us as a guiding force. This is not a power that is to be taken lightly or dismissed as "soft." Wisdom helps us to be very practical and helps us to understand how to hold others accountable. With wisdom, we harbor no ill will, as this is what contaminates us as well as others.

The peace and power of reflection was brought home to us once again following the events of September 11. I always appreciated the power of reflection as a place for insights, for practical knowledge on how to live my life in harmony. I never fully realized how much peace of mind reflection brings.

After the grief and sadness the American people and much of the world experienced following the September 11 event, a couple of weeks later we felt compelled to follow our instinct and sought succor by going camping at Big Bear Lake, a peaceful area a few hours from Los Angeles. We felt the need to be "ordinary" again, not terrorist victims.

We rediscovered the joy in just living, doing the simple things—roasting frankfurters over a campfire, smelling the fragrance of the wood fire, going for long walks, smelling the fresh scent of pine forest. We saw stars at night that we hadn't observed in years and marveled at the beauty of the universe. Los Angeles has too many city lights to see many stars. We felt at peace and lived in the moment. When we arrived home, that peace continued.

We watched a television news program where Rudy Giuliani, the mayor of New York, was interviewed. He was asked how he managed to be so calm and strong, such a great leader at a time like this. The interviewer mentioned that the mayor was being talked about as "Winston Churchill in a baseball cap." Rudy chuckled at this and related that he admired the ability of the English people to do what they had to do to protect themselves in bomb shelters as they were being bombed during the war. He said that Churchill played a valuable role in reminding the English people to just live and go about their business, despite England being bombed every day. "We will persevere," Churchill said. Giuliani agreed, "We will persevere."

Some questions that occurred to me after reflection are these: What would happen if we used the funds that are being used to mobilize troops and prepare for war, to help those poverty stricken, war ravaged countries, rather than make war on them? What would happen if we asked them how we could help them, in their way, not how *we* think they need to be helped?

Naive? Perhaps, but on a much smaller scale, this is what has been done successfully in poverty stricken, crime-ridden communities across America. Amidst distrust, skepticism and apathy, the flame of wisdom was lit to illuminate practical solutions to community problems. Why not try this in these countries? Surely there are small groups of people already within these countries who are looking for more than basic survival; clean water, food, shelter, roads, electricity, whatever they feel is important to them. No doubt others would follow as they saw their neighbors have an easier life without losing their dignity, self-respect, culture or religious faith.

If we say that everyone is born with wisdom and common sense, and that the principles of Mind, Consciousness and Thought underlie every human experience, why wouldn't this work with these countries? Again, has it ever been tried?

One of the most important factors we discovered in our community work here in America is understanding that everyone *does* have wisdom. And that when we talked to that wisdom in people, they responded. True, it took some time and not everyone responded. But time after time, community after community, inevitably, some people were touched by their own wisdom and began to change.

As they changed, their community changed. People of different ethnic backgrounds and religions came together and worked cooperatively to help each other and their community. These same people had fought and distrusted each other before they understood the wisdom that resides before culture and religion. They began to see that they didn't lose their culture when they respected others' cultures. It only helped them appreciate all cultures more. They began to see that wisdom levels the playing field and brings equality.

During a multi-cultural seminar in Switzerland the video *Applications—Health Realization in the Community* (Lone Pine Publishing) was shown. This video shows people from all walks of life—staff and clients from homeless shelters, counselors and clients from drug and alcohol treatment centers, educators working with inmates in jails, teachers with children in schools, police officers with residents and youth in disadvantaged communities, doctors and nurses in clinics—all working together, all respecting each other as equals. The point of equality touched everyone who attended the seminar. They had never seen anything like this before. The evidence of love and respect could not be denied.

At this time in history, there seems such a need for peace and reflection. We cannot set out to change the world. We can only change ourselves.

> *When I was young and free and my imagination had*
> *no limits,*
> *I dreamed of changing the world.*
> *As I grew older and wiser, I realized the world would*
> *not change.*
> *And I decided to shorten my sights somewhat and*
> *change only my country.*
> *But it too seemed immovable.*
>
> *As I entered my twilight years, in one last desperate*
> *attempt,*
> *I sought to change only my family, those closest to me.*
> *But alas they would have none of it.*

And here now I lie in my deathbed and realize,
Perhaps for the first time, that if only I had changed
myself first,
Then by example I may have influenced my family and
With their encouragement and support I may have bet-
tered my country,
and who knows, I may have changed the world.

—attributed to an Anglican bishop
(about 1100 AD)

Reflection: Being in the Moment

Reflection allows Mind to express wisdom through the individual. Reflection stills personal thinking so that original thought can be heard, recognized and put to use. There is no ritual or technique to prompt or hasten the process. The only requirement is being in the moment, enjoying and appreciating life. Then, as if out of nowhere, inspiration occurs.

Recently, a friend shared his insight with me. "I've realized how much more powerful it is to be reflective rather than talk about reflection, to be peaceful rather than talk about being peaceful, to be in the moment rather than talk about being in the moment. Wisdom reveals itself in those moments when you least expect it."

I asked my friend to tell me more. "I was given an opportunity," he said, "to conduct a seminar for a group who had little or no understanding of the power of the principles. I was excited but at the same time felt somewhat insecure. My personal thinking kept up a running stream of "what if" thoughts. Every time I noticed this I did the best I could to just let those thoughts pass.

"Finally, the big day arrived and to my eternal gratitude I forgot about my anxiety and was able to be in the moment with the group. This allowed me to listen and really hear what was important to them, to hear how I could bridge the gap between what they knew and what I knew.

"Being in the moment allowed me to respond to them in a way I hadn't experienced before. Questions occurred to me that drew out *their* wisdom and many of them had insights in the moment. Questions occurred to them as well and most of the time, they would come up with answers to their own questions. It was a wonderful process of exploration and discovery, a dynamic and enriching experience.

"I realized that I didn't have to 'entertain' them, that simply being in touch with my wisdom helped activate their wisdom. It was a remarkable occasion. I never knew how practical wisdom is. Wisdom seemed more of a philosophy and usually someone else's philosophy. I never gave much credence to the fact that we all have the capacity for original thought. This helped me see that all people would benefit by this understanding. It would help different ethnicities respect each others' differences rather than fight over them. Then there could be real and meaningful dialogue, without either side thinking they were losing face. This experience really opened my eyes and I'm very grateful."

My friend's story touched me. I could feel his gratitude for what he had discovered. Clearly, his understanding of the potential of human beings relating to one another at a deeper level had been enhanced as a result of his insight. His skill as a facilitator had also been enhanced by his discovery, increasing his sensitivity to the need to encourage the unfolding of the participants' wisdom rather than holding center stage himself.

All too often people confuse the message of hope that this understanding offers with the messenger. They think certain people have "charisma" and may get excited and hopeful during the seminar conducted by this person. Usually this feeling is only temporary, not of lasting value, because they look to the "charismatic" individual as having the answer and not themselves. How wonderful that my friend has discovered the true joy of seeing people uncover their own wisdom, which once uncovered is never lost.

Another point comes to mind regarding the value of living in and appreciating the moment rather than being concerned about the past and future. During a coaching session, a client related his distress about a situation that had occurred with a close friend. A difference of opinion had created unpleasant feelings between them.

"I realize living in the moment is a good thing most of the time," my client said, "but what about those times when you are gripped by negative thoughts? It's difficult to let those thoughts go, especially when you feel you are in the right," he stated indignantly. "When I'm having negative thoughts, they are thoughts I'm having in the moment. I don't like those feelings but I can't let them go."

"Everyone has times like that," I responded, "but you just said something important about feelings. What was that you said?"

He pondered for a moment then replied, "I don't know; something about not liking negative feelings."

"When do you feel those negative feelings?"

"When I'm thinking negative thoughts, of course! I keep trying to let them go, but those same specific thoughts keep coming back and I know I'm taking it personally but I can't seem to get out of it."

"Perhaps you're thinking too much," I replied.

We took a break and decided to go for a walk in the park. Changing the subject, I asked him about his grandson and we chatted enjoyably for a time then stopped to observe some squirrels busily gathering and storing nuts.

His face had cleared of tension considerably by this time. As we sat on a park bench, idly enjoying doing nothing, he suddenly spoke. "It just occurred to me that I haven't been thinking about the altercation with my friend. I feel so much better, like a weight is lifted off my shoulders. I realize that I was focusing on my personal thinking and the more I tried to fight it, the more I became gripped.

"It's amazing," he marveled, "when you get centered again and simply enjoy the moment, wisdom occurs. I feel like I see my friend's side of things now and understand better where I got off track. Even if my friend and I still don't see eye to eye on things, it doesn't really matter. I understand and respect his right to his opinion. We can agree to disagree and still be friends, but somehow I know we'll be fine. It's so simple that I can't understand how I failed to grasp it before!"

The Quiet Defusing of Stress

A couple of weeks ago a friend asked me to write something about stress, and specifically, stress in the workplace. As I was feeling some stress and tension at the time she asked me, I didn't feel particularly inspired to write about this topic. Nonetheless, the thought was planted and I resolved to see what occurred to me during my own experience of stress.

Simply stated, nothing occurred to me but silence. I felt most comfortable when I wasn't dwelling on the specifics of the situation that I was in the throes of experiencing. When another friend called, I took the opportunity to ask him for advice and mentioned that I was feeling impatient with the progress of an individual. As I spoke with my friend, I could hear that I was feeling invested in the outcome of this particular situation and it became humorous to me. Still, I found myself wavering between humor and impatience. It was like riding a roller coaster.

My friend said something that really made sense to me. He reminded me that when the feeling is off-center in a relationship, "you are moving sideways, not forward, and you want to stop and wait for harmony and goodwill before proceeding." When he made that statement it stopped me in my tracks and in that stopping, the resiliency of wisdom had an opportunity to appear.

I saw once again that when insecurity raises its head, you go back to old habits of thinking and behavior. It's like finding and waving an old pair of dirty socks in the air. You wonder where on earth they came from! The old habits of thinking feel uncomfortable, tired and smelling of the past. When you are in the middle of an attack of insecurity, it is so tempting to address the specifics that you *think* are the cause of the insecurity.

Instead, I discovered how powerful and helpful it is to keep the tongue silent in the middle of discord, that this quiet can settle and defuse the tension so that harmony prevails. This is when answers and understanding appear. Learn to trust this spiritual process and harmony will resolve the specific details. It is like turning down the heat under a pressure cooker; it takes the pressure off all parties concerned.

The quiet silence I am talking about is a comfortable silence, peaceful in its nature. It is being at home in the center of your universe, in touch with Mind. There are different qualities of silence, as was pointed out to me recently by a respected elder of the Wampanoag tribe. We had the opportunity to spend some time with the author of a book about the history of the Wampanoag tribe. She resonated with the principle of Mind and related it to the Great Spirit, the creator of all things. She spoke of silences that aren't always productive and how these can be awkward and uncomfortable. She also spoke of other silences that are warm and rich and provide a nurturing foundation for insights.

I observed the nurturing quality of just such a silence at a seminar. As the facilitator asked for comments or insights to be shared, a beautiful, warm feeling of goodwill developed. One by one, people shared what they had learned during the seminar. The feeling deepened and there were long, quiet moments that were rich and nourishing. Then a man spoke about a recent tragedy and about how he had handled it with equanimity, surprising himself at the time, and feeling very grateful. The silence and feeling of goodwill continued. Others spoke and still the harmony was in place. Then another person started to "teach" how she had handled tragedy in the past, and the feeling lessened. Someone else spoke and shared something in the moment and the feeling picked up again.

The facilitator ended the session for lunch, but before she did that, she asked that we notice the power of silence, how silence can be healing, and that sometimes words get in the way of the silence. "When we listen to someone sharing a story about a sad event, if there is no attachment to the story, but simply relating in a positive manner what they've learned from the event, then you want to be aware of the feeling. If it's positive, then let the feeling carry on. You don't need to add anything else."

The woman who had tried to "teach" what she had learned was grateful to realize that it wasn't necessary to teach, that in this particular case, the silence was the teacher. She realized that when she had first shared with another group what she had learned about understanding stress, it was when they were overwhelmed by a tragic event that had taken place. At that time, what she shared in the moment was helpful to the group. This time, when she "taught" what she had learned, it was from memory. No one was overwhelmed so it wasn't necessary to add anything, just to listen. She also saw that it is best to teach in the moment, not from the past.

This insight gave her great relief. She saw that she didn't need to "teach" as much as "listen" and that listening creates a healing silence. There is an old saying:

You were born with one mouth and two ears
So that you could listen twice as much as talk.

A CEO related this story to me. "Until I understood how the principles generate the human experience, I always believed that stress was created from the outside in, so I would blame or try and change the external circumstances. Never did I consider that my thinking had anything to do with the stress I was experiencing.

"I thought the stress was a result of my employees not being responsible for getting the job done, or budget hassles, lack of leadership among the executive team, and a variety of other reasons. I had problems delegating because I felt that no one could do the job as well as I could or as fast as I could, so why bother. If I did delegate a project to someone, I would approach the busiest person in the office, someone who had a desk piled high with work, because I felt that they were productive. I would not approach anyone whose desk was clear and who looked relaxed and at ease because I felt they were lackadaisical and not productive and would put off doing today what could be done tomorrow.

"Once I realized how wisdom works and that stress is created from the inside out, it turned my life upside down, or you might say, inside out. Understanding that thought flows moment to moment allowed me to let the stressful thoughts flow out of my consciousness, and healthy thoughts took their place. This understanding not only changed my life but also had a positive impact on my employees. I listen more and talk less. I delegate more and stress less. My employees are empowered like never before, taking responsibility, getting more creative and demonstrating leadership in ways I never expected. There is significantly less stress in the whole company and the bottom line is everyone is happier in their work and we've never looked better financially. Clearly, stress doesn't pay."

Thought Flows—If You Let It

The remarkable nature of the principle of Thought continues to awe me with its neutrality and, at the same time, its capacity to flow. Thought has no power on its own, without us giving it a personal framework to fit into, by the content of our thinking. This incredible birthright that human beings have seems to be virtually ignored or unknown by much of the world. Yet it is such a gift to know that we have the power within us to create our experience of life, simply by thinking. It is such a benefit to know that thought flows, so that we never have to keep our past alive, unless we choose to, by thinking old thoughts.

This capacity to think and the nature of thought flowing brought tremendous relief to a group of homeless and substance abuse clients at a drug and alcohol treatment center located on skid row in Los Angeles. Some of the staff at the center are conducting principles-training for the clients and residents of the area. Our group of trainees had the opportunity to visit and conduct a daylong training for this treatment center. For many of our trainees, it was the first time they had ever been in a skid row area.

The day started off with the group that we were invited to train not being available, and we were told that they were not expecting us at all. Our group simply absorbed this information and went with the "flow." Then we were told that perhaps another department of the drug and alcohol treatment center may have a client group for us to talk with so we all trooped down the street to visit this department. We must have looked somewhat out of place, as our trainees were very clearly not from skid row. Although dressed casually in jeans and T-shirts, we were all clutching water bottles and walking in a rather large group. Nevertheless, people on the streets gave us a cursory glance, and then went on with their day.

When we arrived at the screening and evaluation center, again there was no group ready for us. While I was discussing the probability of whether a group would become available, our trainees began talking with a man who happened to be walking by. When the man found out that our group was trained in the principles, he enthusiastically began to share with them his discovery of this understanding and the impact this knowledge has had on his life. Our group was entranced and deeply touched by him and his wisdom.

We were offered a tour of the homeless drop-in center about a block away and while we were on the tour the staff said they would gather a group together for our trainees to talk with. A kind young woman, a member of the staff, chatted about her understanding of the principles as she escorted us to the drop-in center. As we walked together, a street woman approached her and asked her for a hug. The young woman immediately stopped and embraced the street woman with much warmth. Several residents of the street called out greetings to us as we passed, saying "God bless you." Our group responded in kind.

We were given a tour of the drop-in center. I had been there before on a regular basis and was delighted to talk with staff that had gone through our training almost three years earlier. As we stood in the courtyard absorbing the warm community feeling, I asked the staff how this understanding had helped them in their work at the center. One woman responded, "Just listening to our guests is healing to them. They don't often get people who will take the time to listen. When we listen to them, they appreciate it so much that many times they will come back for more help."

The staff also mentioned how much the understanding of how we create our experience helped them to not get gripped by the chaotic situations in which they often find themselves. Knowing that thought flows allows them to not entertain negative or worrisome thoughts for too long. They understand that such thoughts cloud their healthy thinking, keeping them from their wisdom and their ability to listen without distraction getting in the way.

As we concluded our tour and started our walk back to the treatment center to see if there was a group for us to talk with, a male staff member walked with us. One of our trainees asked him how he introduced the principles to the clients and guests of the drop-in center. He said, "I talk to them about another way of looking at Thought, and how to find well-being inside themselves. Then I explain how Mind, Consciousness and Thought create our experience of life and how we have a choice to use these principles to create either a heaven on earth or a hell." His words touched us deeply and moved us to silence.

He carried with him a copy of our *Health Realization Primer*. It was tattered and dog-eared from much use. He said, "This book saved my life. Before my job here, I was on the streets too, and one of the people you trained, trained me. He's my mentor and he gave me a copy of this book. It showed me what we have inside of us, that I was healthy inside. I've never looked back. Now I am helping others." Again, we were silent, too moved to speak.

When we arrived at the treatment center, we found almost 30 people waiting for us, mainly men and also two women, many of them fresh off the streets and some still ridding their system of drugs and alcohol. Perhaps six of them had heard something about the principles and to the rest, it was new information.

After I introduced our group and said a few words, I turned the program over to the trainees and went to the back of the room. The trainees did a fine job sharing what the principles meant to them and talked about the changes in their lives. The new people were bewildered. They saw the trainees as people who were "normies," not addicts, and were uncertain how they could help when the trainees didn't understand addiction. One man said, "We're confused, but your smiling faces are keeping us here. We want to know what you know."

One young trainee spoke up very clearly, acknowledging that although she was not addicted to drugs or alcohol, she was addicted to thoughts of insecurity and gave examples of how those thoughts messed up her life. Other trainees spoke of thought as the key to understanding the past and of how they had realized that we have the ability to let those thoughts go, that the very nature of Thought is flowing.

As the foundation of this understanding was laid, and the principles shared, the feeling in the room deepened, the questions lessened and the audience became more attentive. At one point, the trainees broke the participants into small groups. I left the room and wandered back to the staff room where I talked with a couple of men who had been in the training earlier. They mentioned how struck they were by the trainees, how the trainees' normality gave them a fresh look at what they themselves were looking for. "We've forgotten what it's like to live without chemicals to make us feel good. These people seem to feel good without drugs! We want to know how they do that."

When I went back into the training room, the small-group conversations were animated. The guests and the trainees were each sharing what they were discovering in the moment. Clearly there was mutual respect and rapport between the groups. Gone was the feeling of confusion and of wondering how each group could relate to the other. The spiritual nature of the human spirit had been released and acknowledged as the common meeting ground. When we left, each group was reluctant to part and the participants were saying, "When will you be back?"

I was impressed by many things that day. First of all, the trainees had risen to the occasion admirably. They were unfazed by the fact that there wasn't a group to talk with when we arrived. They remained in the moment, ready for whatever came. They listened with respect to whomever they met and treated people with dignity and equality. Even when there was confusion during the early part of the training, they maintained their bearings and carried on. They were genuinely touched by what they heard from the staff and the guests and recognized the wisdom that emerged from them.

What impressed me about the guests of the treatment center was their courtesy and kindness to us. They weren't expecting us, had been given a pass in the morning to go and do errands, and then had arrived back at the center to have the rest of the day off. Instead, they were met by their caseworker, stating that they were to attend our training. Understandably, some resisted the idea. Still, they attended and were gracious and kept the comments to a minimum.

They saw that here was a group of people who were not addicts or in recovery coming to talk to them. The event was unusual and yet they listened. The guests were confused by the information and the stories that were being shared. One guest became frustrated by this and finally raised his hand to state, "I don't want to hurt your feelings or offend you, but I don't know what the hell you're talking about!" But he remained gracious and was obviously concerned that he not hurt our feelings by his statement. Our group found this remarkable.

It seems to me that rapport, listening and goodwill played an enormous part in the success of this event. The ability to let thought flow played an equally important role in staying in the moment, being unfazed by whatever occurred and feeling protected, despite the unusual circumstances. The principles inherent in human beings, that create our experience moment to moment, were demonstrated that day, to everyone's benefit. It was a memorable and unforgettable experience.

The Y Analogy

Isn't it amazing that we use the same universal energy, Mind, to create panic or calm, dissatisfaction or gratitude, confusion or understanding? When you reflect on this spiritual fact, it opens the door to a whole new world, simplifying the creation of our reality.

Look at the stem of the letter "Y" and see the stem as yourself, then look at the "V" above the stem and see that as the fork in the road, the choice an individual has—to be calm or panicked, to be grateful or dissatisfied, to have understanding or be confused.

All choices are rooted in thought and thought creates feelings and emotions, feelings and emotions that are healthy or that are less healthy. Ask yourself what you would rather have, the feeling of calm or of panic, the feeling of gratitude or of dissatisfaction, the feeling of understanding or of confusion? Clearly, most of us would prefer the positive feeling.

But how do you attain these positive feelings, you might ask? When you are in the middle of an "anxiety" attack, your thoughts are very compelling. How do you move out of those thoughts?

The beauty is that thoughts flow like a river, taking our anxiety, dissatisfaction and confusion with it once we understand that the nature of thought is flowing. When we appreciate the feeling of gratitude, that feeling brings contentment and peace of mind, no matter the circumstances. The feeling of gratitude clears the thought-river of debris, allowing the current of wisdom to run freely, providing answers and solutions to difficulties that we may experience in life.

We want to connect the feelings we experience with the fact that we are the thinker, that our thoughts create feelings, all kinds of feelings—not just the good feelings but the less pleasant feelings too. We want to appreciate the power of seeing that we are the thinker. Too often people give their power away by saying, "I feel this way because my plans have gone awry." Or "I feel like this because I didn't get the promotion I was promised." Or "I feel this way because I have no money."

Those thoughts are conditional thoughts that can end up controlling you. Realize that Thought as a principle is neutral, universal energy and that by the act of thinking, we form that energy into our personal reality. Then we are back in the driver's seat of our life, driving down the bumpy road of unrest or the smooth lane of harmony.

It doesn't matter what thoughts we think. Forget trying to figure out which thought is behind the feeling or "Y" we are thinking those thoughts. Just *realize* that you are the thinker. This is all you need to do. ***The act of observing yourself as the thinker has the power to change the reaction you experience.*** This is an incredibly helpful thing to know.

A colleague related this story. "I've had panic attacks for five years. It got so bad that I couldn't leave my home to visit my friends or family. If I went shopping, I would experience such panic that I had to rush out of the mall. When I first learned about the principles I longed to believe them. But I continued to experience panic. I kept studying the principles to see how feelings were created but I couldn't connect the principles to me.

"I thought my feelings came from the situation. When I was in the mall, I thought the feeling of panic came from all the people jostling about. When I was driving down the street to visit my family, I thought the panic came from driving on the freeway with all the vehicles rushing at me. It was terrifying but I forced myself to continue. Sometimes it got better but I still had the panic attacks.

"Then I talked to my counselor who first introduced me to the principles and he helped me realize that I was my own worst enemy, that I was using the principles against myself. Up to that point, I thought that you 'applied' the principles, that you had to practice them daily. I didn't realize that we are the principles in motion all the time. When that dawned on me, it changed my life. Now I can go out and truly enjoy myself.

"Occasionally, when my personal thoughts take over and I start to panic again, I find myself able to regain my equilibrium much quicker. I also find myself more appreciative of my own inner strength. Before, I used to think it was ego to think of oneself as strong and resourceful but now I see the difference between ego and confidence. They *feel* very different."

Another story illustrates the power of understanding. A friend of mine, John, is a financial planner. When I first met him he told me that he was an overachiever and that he believed that was what had led to his financial success. John seemed rather proud of this ability. He told me that his father had died when John was a young man and that as an only child he had taken on the role of the man of the house to help his mother. He felt a tremendous responsibility to take care of his mother and for this he dedicated many years of his life to ensure that his mother was amply provided for.

His work ethic was stringent and he worked long hours and often through the weekend. He also volunteered much of his time to sit on charitable committees and foundation boards to be of service to others. He found it increasingly difficult to relax and began to drink heavily. He struggled with insomnia.

I gave him Sydney Banks' book, *The Enlightened Gardener*. He told me that reading that book started his introspection on what he was doing with his life. He began to realize that there was more to life than being financially successful.

"What good is financial success when I'm not happy?" he asked rhetorically. " I know there's more to life than that because my financial resources aren't bringing me content-ment like I thought they would. I am amazed that I'm having to learn how to relax. I've been so wound up that it's not been easy to slow down. However, I have resigned several of my positions on various committees and I find I'm doing a much better job for the ones with which I continue to work. I'm far more attentive and have better ideas on how to help.

"My insomnia is easing up and I am starting to get more sleep. I find myself making wiser choices with what I do with my down time, realizing that I deserve some time for myself, that I'm more productive in every aspect of my life when I respect my own inner health. I'm even working out again. I wish I had known about these principles ten years ago. I might have saved my marriage."

Draw your own conclusions from these stories. Calm or panic? Gratitude or dissatisfaction? Understanding or confu-sion? You have the power and the ability to make the wise choice.

Follow Your Dream

Occasionally, when people hear the phrase "follow your dream," they may think it's referring to a romanticized notion of living happily ever after. For me, following your dream means this: following the feeling, listening to the feeling and allowing your wisdom to manifest.

How many times have you had a gut feeling to move forward on some decision, or a visceral feeling that it was best to wait for a time until something became clear. All of this pondering is grounded in thought and feeling. Some of you will recognize that you had such a moment but perhaps ignored it. Yet when questioned, you might say, "Yes, I remember when I felt that I should do this or that, and when I did trust that feeling, it worked out. When I didn't, I wished I had."

In the past, I used to dream of things I desired for my life, material goals and objectives. I dreamed of living in Hawaii, of having a good job that paid well, of a marriage that always remained loving and exciting. I dreamed that my children would be happy and successful.

All my dreams seemed to be related to desires and when they didn't turn out, I was disappointed and discontented. I thought it was my lot in life not to think above myself. That was when I didn't understand the power of Thought and when I didn't trust that the unknown future could be better than your dreams or desires.

What is it about Thought that can pave the way to follow your dream? Let me give you an example. For some time, Ken and I had a strong feeling it was time to leave the Los Angeles area. We felt that our work there was done, and as we reflected on this feeling, we realized that our work could be accomplished anywhere. The business travel, training and coaching we do requires that we be near a major airport and a phone. That is easy to arrange.

The next thing that came clear to us was that we wanted to be nearer our family, that we were missing the best years of watching our grandchild grow up. We missed our son and daughter, and Ken's mother was becoming increasingly frail. We also wanted to be in a quieter location, with clean air and a more rural environment.

The first thing we did was list our home for sale. We didn't know where we were going but felt this was the first step. It felt right to do this, so we followed the feeling. Our home sold within the week, for the price we wanted. Things looked good but now we needed to get a move on and find our new home.

We still weren't sure where to move, but Salt Spring Island, one of the Gulf Islands off the coast of B.C. near Vancouver, was beckoning us. It was where we had started our journey of self-discovery and it had a strong draw for us. Our family was close by so everything seemed right.

We made arrangements to fly to Vancouver and from there we took the ferry to the island to find our new home. We found our home within three days, with a wonderful ocean view, and made an offer, conditional on the completion of sale on our Long Beach home. Our offer was accepted.

The future looked very promising and we were elated. In my mind I was positioning the furniture in our new home, wondering how the sofa would look on this wall, where we could fit the china cabinet, and discussing with Ken the probability of redoing the facing on the fireplace. All was right with the world and we were in seventh heaven.

One week later, in the midst of our packing, boxes strewn all over the house, wrapping paper coming out of our ears, we got a call from our realtor informing us that the deal on our Long Beach home had fallen through. Consequently, our offer on our new home fell through because we couldn't meet the down payment for the property.

Our dream came crashing down around our ears, shattering our hopes and giving us pause to question our faith. We had followed the feeling; we had done everything right; what happened?

For a day or two, I tried to do everything I could to save our new property, discussing loans, lines of credit, anything that came to mind. My husband cautioned me to be patient; saying things would turn out for the best. I agreed—then continued to try and think of something, anything, to prevent losing our new home.

Finally, in a moment of mental exhaustion, my circular thinking quietened and wisdom emerged. I *realized* that Ken was right. Peace came over me and I settled down to live my life in the moment, trusting that what was meant to be, would be. There were moments when nagging thoughts came. What if? Could we do this? Could we do that? Then peace came again. It was an interesting time of seeing another level of "follow your dream." It wasn't *push* your dream, it was *follow* your dream. The difference had eluded me.

Now, following your dream, for me, means living in the moment, trusting in the unknown, and letting the future unfold at its own pace, not my pace. I discovered that following your dream is a birthright, not a desire. It is living your dream, content that the future will unfold in the way it is meant.

Once I settled down in my thinking, the future unfolded beautifully. Our house in Long Beach resold two weeks after the first deal fell through. The offer was financially better, allowing us to recoup the extra trips we had taken to the island. We found our new home and it was definitely better than the one we had lost. It feels good, it feels peaceful and life goes on, living the dream.

Living Your Dream

"Living your dream" isn't what I imagined it would be. I had visions of effortlessly sailing through life's changes as Ken and I prepared to leave Long Beach, which had been our home for five years, and follow our dream of moving to Salt Spring Island.

It has been a revelation to see how many hidden expectations are contained in the desire to "live your dream." Expectations that limit your ability to enjoy life as it is unfolding, thoughts that prevent you from seeing and appreciating new opportunities because these opportunities did not appear in your original dream.

When Ken and I left Long Beach, we were following a strong feeling that this was the right direction for us. We had no idea what the future held but most of the time enjoyed being in the moment, content that the future would take care of itself and, for the most part, trusting that if we were in harmony with life, life would be kind.

As we left Los Angeles, Ken driving the moving van, towing his Explorer on a trailer behind, and me following in my car, I felt joy and lightness and found a smile growing on my face that would not leave. We had a wonderful journey traveling across California, and were in awe as Mount Shasta, covered in snow, rose majestically in the distance. Then Oregon, where to our great delight, we saw our first logging truck. We drove through the state of Washington, with Mount Rainier luring us onward, and soon we were arriving at Peace Arch Park, with the border crossing at Blaine just outside of Bellingham. Customs officers were friendly, didn't check our possessions at all, just welcomed us home, and we were on the final lap of our journey.

During our trip we took each moment as it came, and everything flowed. However, once we got to our destination, Salt Spring Island, subtle expectations began to creep in and life was not as smooth. We arrived at our new home and were thrilled with it but had to wait a considerable time until we were able to move in. Business projects that were scheduled had to be delayed or cancelled.

Life threw us a few curve balls and because of expectations that everything should unfold smoothly, my eyes weren't on the ball. They were closed, daydreaming, and so I couldn't see the benefits of not being able to move into our new home right away or of having no projects to do. I couldn't see the benefits, such as having time for a good rest, being fortunate to have found a cozy cottage overlooking a lovely lake, having the time to contemplate and to write. All I could see was that we weren't able to move into our new home and that work wasn't unfolding as planned.

In a short while, the feeling of peacefulness and gratitude emerged again and allowed me to see more clearly. My husband had time for his hobby of tying flies and fishing for trout on the lake in front of the cottage. We had time to enjoy long walks in the woodlands and beaches on the island, time to find a fern hollow to explore and time to marvel at the beauty and mystical feeling pervading the hollow. Yes, to follow your dream can be inspirational and propel you forward but to live life in the moment can take you beyond your dream, to the unknown realm full of possibilities never dreamt of before.

A client mentioned that he was puzzled that he continued to experience the occasional struggle in life. "Why is it that I experience the beauty of life for a time and then it seems to disappear? I thought that now that I understand how the principles work, life should be easy and there shouldn't be any struggle."

How many times have you heard this comment from others or thought that way yourself? It's a common question but when I heard it from my client at this particular moment, with what I had been experiencing myself, the earnest question made me laugh. What popped into my mind was something Sydney Banks has said many times.

"***Life is a contact sport.***"

That statement is so profound. If you really hear it, it takes away all the pressure, all expectations, all judgment, and allows you to live life and to enjoy all the novel and interesting aspects of life as a contact sport. You learn, through your own wisdom, guided by your feelings, how to play the game of life as a contact sport, with skill, gentleness and appreciation.

Realizing that life is a contact sport allows you to relax and to not judge yourself or others. But just because you now understand something about how life works doesn't mean that you will never experience struggle again. This understanding allows the "struggle" to flow out of your thoughts. It's only when you think life should be perfect, without any glitches, that you set yourself up for a fall and that your thoughts become circular, rather than flowing.

When I mentioned this statement, "life is a contact sport," to my client, he burst out laughing and we both went into gales of laughter. He was so relieved to realize that the purpose of life is to learn from each contact and to find it interesting that each contact keeps moving you forward.

When we become immersed in expectations, we become stationary, with blinders on, and we are prevented from seeing the unknown blossom into the known, from seeing impossibilities turn into possibilities. How fascinating life is with all its ups and downs. How blessed we are to know what creates those ups and downs. Yes, follow your dream but don't forget to live your life in the moment.

Different Worlds—
Same Understanding

Basel, Switzerland is a charming, medieval town and one of my favorite places. I feel at home there and have spent many wonderful hours strolling along the Rhine River. The Rhine flows from east to north dividing *Grossbasel* (Greater Basel) from *Kleinbasel* (Lesser Basel). Exploring the host of medieval churches and the historic Old Town with its many winding side streets lined with 16th-century townhouses is a favorite pastime.

It was a privilege for me to spend some time working in Basel with people who were learning to facilitate and teach others about the principles of human development. I first went to Basel in April 2001 and met many fine people who were eager to learn about an understanding that has a simple, profound power to change one's life. I've been there three times and each time I see that the people who have engaged their wisdom are not only changing their lives, but also influencing others. It is truly an honor to see this process unfold and touch an ever-growing group of interested people.

There were several different nationalities represented in this group who had come together to participate in our program, including Swiss, German, Israeli, Danish, English and Canadian. The diversity of this group provided a richness of cultural differences that was fascinating and enlightening to everyone.

Some of the people knew each other from previous programs but many were new to each other. We spent two weekends together, four short days. In that time, we began to know each other and grow together in understanding. We saw how people with very different backgrounds can come together in harmony, appreciating and celebrating the differences and open to and respecting how, under the skin, we're essentially the same.

One person might speak of Universal Mind, another of God, or Universal Wisdom, Flow of Energy, Oneness, and all would know we were talking about the same spiritual power, expressed in different terms. This understanding brought fusion to the group, an openness and curiosity that led to deep exploration of how each participant saw life, an openness to moving into the unknown, eager to learn more.

There was an understated but powerful sense of encouragement and support for each person, trusting that the unknown would unfold in a way that was appropriate for each individual. There was no pressure to take a position on how much or what a person knew; rather an acceptance of everyone's reality and of everyone's wisdom. People built on one another's insights, strengthening the foundation of shared wisdom so that everyone was stronger and richer in their combined knowledge.

In the beginning, if someone was rather hesitant about sharing their understanding, the feeling of safety and encouragement gently prompted them to open up. Insights flowed from many and illuminated all who were present.

During the program, we played a videotape illustrating the impact of principle-based programs in the justice system. Featured on the video was the commander of a prison who stated that he was skeptical at the beginning of the program, doubting that the inmates who were imprisoned for murder, rape and other felonies would learn anything. To his surprise, the inmates who attended these classes began to change. They calmed down, were less frustrated, required less discipline and were more compassionate toward the corrections officers.

One man on the videotape, imprisoned for life, spoke in a matter-of-fact way of the value of having the same training for the COs (corrections officers), stating that he could see that the officers were under a great deal of stress, and how nice it would be for them to realize the connection between stress and thought. He noted that if the officers learned this, it would help them in their home life as well. One of our program participants whispered, "They would be called 'compassionate officers' rather than 'corrections officers'."

Different worlds—same understanding. A commander of a prison and an inmate seeing that people can change, from the inside out. Seeing that it is *never* too late. Imagine if other leaders in correction facilities and the justice system began to realize these principles.

During my stopover in London's Heathrow Airport, I read in the newspaper of the difficulties the police chiefs and the justice system are experiencing in Great Britain. One of the top government officials was berating the police chiefs for lack of leadership and innovative programs. The article also mentioned that staff in some jails were refusing to release prisoners who should have been released, because the staff didn't agree with the policy of early release. Imagine if staff and inmates were given the opportunity to release their wisdom and creativity.

Imagine if leaders in countries around the world could come together in the same manner described earlier in this chapter: coming together in understanding, building on each other's ideas, appreciating and celebrating the differences in cultures, open to and respecting how all mankind is the same spiritual energy. Imagine…different worlds, same understanding.

The Tone Meister

Ever since I began learning about the principles of Mind, Consciousness and Thought, the factor that has helped me the most is understanding that feelings and emotions play a key role in our development as human beings. Up until I gained that understanding, I barely noticed or acknowledged my feelings. When I did notice them I tended to deny my feelings, innocently of course, as I had no knowledge of their value in guiding us through life. I had no idea that feelings act as a directional compass in terms of the quality of our thinking.

I used to be ashamed of my less than noble feelings such as jealousy and envy and defensive about my feelings of indignation and anger when I felt wronged. When I had warm feelings of happiness, contentment and appreciation I attributed them to external circumstances. I had no comprehension that my feelings came from my thinking. I suspect there are many people who experience the same ignorance of the role of feelings in everyday life.

There is a feeling or tone that underlies all human interaction just as there is in the performance of music. In music, the tone of the piece being performed, whether by an individual in a solo performance or by an orchestra, whether playing instruments or using the voice as an instrument, there is a key element of tone that tells whether one is in that place of harmony or out of sync. There is a musical resonance in harmony that can take people to the sublime or in discord that can make everyone feel uncomfortable. So it is with the tone of human interactions.

Tone is an enormously helpful tool, not only in music, but also in life. I learned while I was in Europe that in music, some individuals are called "tone meisters." These are masters at hearing the most subtle nuances of music. A classical singer told me that when she was making a CD and had several cuts of the same song to choose from, she asked the tone meister to help her select the best cut. The tone meister listened for the feeling and the sound that combined the passion and technical skill of the artist to the best advantage.

To me, this is a fascinating aspect of how Mind, as pure energy, works in the physical and spiritual sense. As human beings we have the ability to transform this pure energy into form, whether it is in music or in the dance of interactions with others. You can *hear* the tone of interaction. You can *hear* the tone of engagement, of curiosity, or of disinterest.

In Europe I had the opportunity to listen to several audiotapes of participants in our training program. I had asked them to share their understanding of the principles with an audience and to tape it so we could have dialogue that would help them deepen their understanding. The presentations were spoken in Swiss German and German. I do not understand these languages though I have picked up a few words in my travels.

However, to my surprise and pleasure, I was able to *hear* what was being said beyond the spoken word. I *heard* the tone of the presenter and the audience. I could tell when the presenter was relaxed and confident and I could *hear* when the audience was engaged or disinterested. I could *hear* when the silence was rich or when the silence was awkward.

This marvelous experience was very helpful in deepening my trust in the tone or feeling of life. The energy that we are made of is resonating all the time, but we are so used to ignoring what the feeling is telling us that we end up shooting ourselves in the foot more often than not, at least until we have a clue as to how the energy is used as a guide to facilitate our journey through life.

Feeling, as energy, has substance, although we cannot see it. Feeling provides safety, which allows us to explore the unknown with confidence, relaxed and trusting in the power of insight and creativity. Feeling allows us to explore the unknown with wisdom, finding originality, rather than doing the impossible by trying to figure it out with our intellect. Feeling also allows us to look at known information and gain a new perspective. This is an example of wisdom and the intellect working in harmony.

There is a distinctly different tone to exploring the known and the unknown with intellect as opposed to exploring with wisdom. Let me give you an example. While I was conducting a team-building session, the group began to explore different ways of collaborating in order to minimize the overlapping of duties between departments. As they began to focus on the details of who was doing what, when and where, the tone began to lag even though the discussion had started out with enthusiasm and eagerness. We had a tone meister in the group who intervened and brought the group back to center. There was a brief pause for reflection, then the meeting carried on, with the focus on the tone and with the patience to see what would happen when people were still for a time;

time for wisdom to emerge, rather than old thinking, old memories.

What happened next was remarkable! As people's wisdom emerged, the energy within the group increased in a subtle way and people began to listen to each other in a more thoughtful and respectful manner. They began building on each other's ideas and more insights occurred. The energy was alive with creativity.

Once you realize that it is your thinking that creates feelings, all types of feelings, you become less reactive to your own thinking and to other people's thinking and behavior. Rather than feeling territorial, you experience compassion, cooperation and collaboration as the norm. You become more productive and effective in your everyday life and in your work.

How wonderful to increase the effectiveness of each of us by becoming "tone meisters." Imagine how our lives, and the lives of those around us, would change if each of us became more conscious of the power of feeling, of the power of Mind.

Point of View or Principle?

Are Mind, Consciousness and Thought a point of view or a set of principles? Do these principles underlying the human experience have the same dependability as the principle of gravity? Is the principle of gravity considered a point of view? Is Einstein's Theory of Relativity considered his point of view? Do the principles work for some and not for others? Does gravity work for some and not for others?

Consideration of these interesting, thoughtful questions can help deepen our understanding of the principles of human experience. When people are first introduced to the three principles, particularly to Thought, they may feel that these principles are similar to other human development theories or programs. Often people claim that they understand that thinking is the solution to our problems. Usually what they are referring to is the content of thinking. If you look closely you will see there are some significant differences.

For example, the difference between the principle of Thought and the content of thinking is a fundamental factor in realizing that we as human beings have the gift to *create* our experience of reality. This means that we are the director of our world, utilizing the power of Mind, Consciousness and Thought in the most productive, healthy way to bring our experience to life.

When we play in the world of content of thinking or personal thinking, we are working with content and behavior that is already created. Some consider this helpful at a behavioral level, but within this process is the opportunity for stress to be activated as we try to change content and behavior from the outside in. There is stressful effort in trying to *do* something to fix yourself or others.

In other words, when people try to change the content of thought and behavior they are trying to change the symptom rather than going directly to the source. Realizing that you are innately healthy, backed up by the power of the principles to create whatever experience you want, productive or nonproductive, is working with the source.

When you see the power and simplicity of Thought as a principle, the unproductive behavior automatically begins to lessen because you are functioning at a healthier level. From that perspective it is easy to see that healthier productive behavior is produced from the inside out.

The principle of Consciousness is the ability to be aware of this process of creating experience. The internal process of Consciousness is very different from the consciousness of outward behavior. When we become externally aware of our behavior and try to change it, we can produce stress by pressuring ourselves to become "better" or achieve more and better goals.

When we become internally conscious that we are the "thinker," we are operating before the formless energy takes on the physical form, through our ability to think. Once again, healthier productive behavior happens automatically, allowing us to *be* better and to become more likely to achieve our goals without stress attached.

Mind is the creative intelligence of *all* things. Mind, as a principle, is more than our brain or personal mind. It is the universal energy behind life, that connects us all together, just as Thought and Consciousness are universal energy. This energy is everywhere, within us and all around us. It is the supreme gift we have been given, enabling us to create our experience of life.

The evidence of these principles at work is a fascinating thing to observe. Each principle is similar to gravity, which is a formless entity holding our world together, in that we can't see gravity but we *feel* its force. It is difficult to describe the principles, just as it is difficult to give an intellectual description of gravity, but this difficulty hasn't stopped us from accepting gravity or observing it at work.

As we start to notice the role of the principles in creating the human experience, we see the evidence unfolding when we see ourselves and others changing, naturally and automatically. This brings to mind the Heisenberg Uncertainty Principle in quantum physics: "The act of observing changes that which is being observed."

Simply by noticing that we are the thinker and not being concerned about *what* we are thinking changes the dynamics of our relationship to life. We become more the observer, participating in life with ease. This understanding gives us added perspective with which to view the diversity of life in all its forms. It liberates us from having to "fix" anyone, knowing that by pointing in the direction of wisdom we provide an opportunity for others to activate their own wisdom and common sense.

A colleague shared an example of this effect from a project meeting she attended. She noticed that others were in a state of anxiety about the project and that the tone of the meeting was producing assumptions that were misleading. She maintained her bearings, not making anything out of it, just noticing the tone. As she put it, "I was able to distinguish mood from intention and let the storm extinguish itself." As the meeting progressed and she maintained her calm, the group started to resonate with that calm energy, creative ideas started to occur and the dynamics completely changed. She was grateful to notice the connection between her state of mind and how it helped defuse the situation.

She also realized afterward that she could have helped shape the tone earlier; she had been aware that some of her colleagues were stressing about the project before the meeting took place. She had sensed the tension but ignored it. This observation gave her food for thought and she knew things would be different next time. She would take the time to talk with people, listen more, establish rapport and good will, and not just move to the task at hand.

Sensing that there is something more than the intellect and moving into the realm of wisdom can sometimes be unnerving. We are so used to operating in the arena of intellect. It is nice to know that as our wisdom deepens, fear dissipates and the intellect and wisdom become partners, operating in harmony.

Business with Heart

Over the years, I've worked in communities and organizations conducting principle-based programs on leadership development, team development and facilitators training courses. Something that continues to touch my heart is how earnest people are about life. No matter what educational, economic or cultural background, most people care a great deal about improving the quality of life for themselves and for others, not just in a material sense but also in a non-material way.

There is talk of wanting better relationships at work and at home. People are seeing other options in life in the way we treat each other, and want to see more trust in and respect for the human spirit and the consideration of a Universal Intelligence that is behind the human spirit.

Occasionally there is conversation of a philosophical or spiritual nature and of an alignment in spirit even if that alignment is expressed using different words or terminology. Perhaps the alignment is not in complete accord, given the different belief systems of humanity. But knowing there is common ground because we all create our experience via the principles of Mind, Consciousness and Thought is an incredible bridge that provides an opportunity to build a foundation on which to hold a meeting of the minds. What a difference in impact on one another when we work from the position of being respectful of our differences and celebrating the common ground. This inclusive attitude opens the door to meaningful conversation and practical results, to business with heart.

A manager at a manufacturing plant related this example. "Scheduling has been a thorn in our side for years. Materials and manufacturing departments weren't working together very well and turf issues developed. When one area came up with an effective schedule they wouldn't share it with the other departments because they were invested in their own success and couldn't see the benefits of involving themselves to help others. Now that they've had some training in seeing healthy high performance as a core competency they are able to see that when the mind is clear they are more open and flexible and can work amicably, sharing information freely. This cooperation is having an impact on the whole division."

An executive coach who was mentoring young executives who were stressing about career decisions shared this story with me. "Usually they come to see me wanting validation for their decisions because they're still uncertain, or perhaps they want me to help them analyze whether it is the right decision. I've noticed that pointing them in the direction of their own wisdom tends to settle them down. Simply reassuring them that they will know what to do and encouraging them to trust their internal feelings as a guidance system about what is important to them helps them make good sound decisions. This way is so much easier than analyzing the decision to the point of total confusion and frustration and finally making the decision based on what is important to the career rather than the individual."

Another manager talked about the assembly plant where he works and the different experience he had when the paint line had to shut down because of faulty skids. "In the past I would have gotten upset and frustrated and would have shouted at employees and generally created more havoc. This time I remained calm, didn't think about 'I have to stay calm,' it just happened. Understanding the role of thought allowed my healthy thinking to emerge during this crisis. I realized that when people are stressed they become less efficient and creative. I knew this before but somehow I didn't walk my talk. My impatience and frustration would come to the surface and I would explode.

"Now my wisdom rose to the occasion. My calmness seemed to help the rest of the team remain calm and we were able to explore other avenues of moving the vehicles with hoists and were able to complete the job. If we had shut down the line for the day, we would have lost approximately a million dollars."

Often I hear people say that it is difficult to introduce the principles to the business world, that you need to prepare people to accept or you must ease into actually presenting the principles. My experience has been that there are various levels of receptivity, in the business world and in all arenas. The business world is not exclusive in regard to considering the validity and practicality of the principles.

What has been most helpful to me when introducing or sharing this understanding is to respect diverse points of view and to find a point of alignment rather than to focus on the differences. The point of alignment usually resides in the recognition that there is a deeper dimension to life. Again, the words to describe this dimension vary but when this discussion happens, a feeling of goodwill occurs that paves the way for a more in-depth conversation. It certainly provides more opportunity to bridge the gap than occurs when challenging the differences.

An example of this was demonstrated very clearly with a mid-management team whose task was to develop a business plan for the following year. It was the first time they had been given the opportunity to do this; in previous years the executive team had developed the business plan. This year the organization was moving toward self-direction, giving all levels of employees more responsibility. To prepare them for this transition the organization provided principle-based culture change programs.

Prior to the culture change programs, the mid-management group had tried to come up with a plan but it turned out to be complex with too many goals and no clear vision for the department. After the culture change program was introduced, which included the concepts of unconditional rapport and deep listening, the business plan came together very well.

When the executive team was invited in to hear the business plan that mid-management had put together, they were pleasantly surprised at the excellent plan, which was simple, with a clear vision, and with fewer goals and tasks assigned. One individual who presented part of the plan said, "As I look at the goals and objectives here on the chart, I can't see any one name on them. This plan is really a blend of all of us." Heads nodded throughout the room. Clearly, ownership involved the whole mid-management team.

The executive team leader, after acknowledging the excellent plan, asked the group, "Why do you think you were able to come up with a plan this time that is so much better, with ownership from all of you?"

Someone spoke out, "We learned about rapport and listening and it seemed to help. There was a good feeling throughout the development of this plan and everyone seemed more respectful of each other." Again, heads nodded throughout the room.

Another member of the executive team, after saying "Well done," asked, "How can we help?"

One of the leaders from mid-management said, "We'll let you know. Right now we have most of the pieces we need and as we get to the areas where we need your help, we'll call."

The executive team member responded, "Great. I guess this allows us more time to develop ourselves and our team. I'll be curious to see how that plays out."

What is so interesting to consider is that these seemingly abstract principles of Mind, Consciousness and Thought produce quantitative results. The business world often asks the question "how does this understanding impact the bottom line?" Hopefully, the above examples illustrate the practicality of the principles and the benefits of doing "business with heart."

Points of Alignment

"Anger is a healthy, natural emotion."
"Women are more nurturing than men."
"Men are more decisive than women."
"It is a cultural issue."
"People are either good or bad; there is no in-between."
"It is either black or white; there is no gray."

These are all "charged" statements. By "charged," I mean they can promote debate, often in an unhealthy manner, in a manner that does not lead to alignment. Debate can be a fascinating exploration of different points of view but my observation is that it can often lead to people becoming even more entrenched in their specific beliefs.

Respectful discussion, on the other hand, often leads to alignment, even when the beliefs are varied and appear oppositional. When statements are made, such as those listed above, it is most helpful to respect the person's point of view even when you don't agree with it.

It's not so much a matter of agreeing or disagreeing but more a matter of understanding—understanding that everyone creates beliefs via thought. This understanding brings a feeling of neutrality, of liberation from judgment and also provides patience and flexibility, less investment in outcome and more interest in simple involvement.

Communication is enhanced because there is genuine interest in how people see life, rather than frustration because of how they see life. This depth of communication happens when you aren't trying to change someone's point of view. This kind of communication happens when a feeling of unconditional rapport is in place, a *knowing* that each person is imbued with wisdom, sometimes covered up, but nonetheless, wisdom still residing in the core of each individual.

Listening for *alignment* rather than for *difference* is also a key element. There will always be a difference of opinion. But how fascinating it is to find a point of alignment and build a relationship upon the foundation of understanding.

For example, take the first statement, "anger is a healthy, natural emotion." For many people the statement is true. For others who see that anger is learned via thought, it is not a true statement. The point of alignment may be that anger is an emotion. Perhaps there may be an exploration and consideration of how anger is created. Is anger created by circumstances, situations and events? Or is anger created by our ability to think? Are situations changed by the way we think about them?

"Women are more nurturing than men." Where is alignment possible in this statement? Perhaps many might agree that women are more nurturing than men. Many may disagree. Could thought have something to do with the common ground that both men and women inhabit? Could both men and women be nurturing?

"Men are more decisive than women." True or false? Where is the point of alignment? Again, does the statement have something to do with the way we think about things; whether individuals know about the potential for certainty, for self-confidence that is hidden deep inside, waiting to be realized?

"It is a cultural issue." This sensitive area often leads to misunderstanding, to the feeling that if you weren't born in a certain culture, then you can't understand its inner workings. Perhaps there is something beyond or underlying culture that also unites mankind. Can we celebrate and appreciate the differences in cultures and also find the common ground within all cultures? Thought brings alignment again. No matter what culture we are a part of, we all are thinkers.

"People are either good or bad; there is no in between." What is remarkable to consider is that all people are born with innate health and with the principles residing within each and every one of us. We have the capacity to create both healthy and unhealthy behavior with the principles we have been gifted with. The essential point is to become aware that we have this gift and can move to whatever behavior we want with the simple recognition that thought creates behavior. Once again thought is the aligning factor.

"It is either black or white; there is no gray." What a drab life it would be were there no colors. All you have to do is look around at the beauty nature has provided, through the universal energy of all things, Mind. Gaze at the sunset filling the sky with the splendor of crimson hues, the gigantic harvest moon, russet gold, reflecting a magic pathway upon the sea.

The ability to see beauty has everything to do with thought. Beauty is in the eye of the beholder. If you see only black or white, perhaps you may miss the color and vibrancy of life. We bring color to our mental state by the various moods we experience. Knowing that moods are created by thought gives us freedom to enjoy the color without taking the black and white too seriously.

Thought, the common denominator, the alignment factor, is something magnificent and powerful to celebrate together. We can clearly see the fact that we all think, and this illustrates the connectedness of mankind. We all think many wonderful, varied thoughts and have various ways of expressing our differences—differences to be enjoyed and contemplated, with the potential of drawing us ever closer, rather than pulling us apart.

Sod's Law

During a recent business trip to England, I heard an intriguing discussion on a morning television talk show. The interviewer was asking a distinguished professor of bio-engineering what he thought about "Sod's Law." I found the term amusing and had no idea what that meant. As I listened to the discussion they clarified that Sod's Law was the same as Murphy's Law that states, "anything that can go wrong will go wrong."

As the discussion continued, the professor pointed out that, in his opinion, Sod's Law was nothing more than cause and effect. The interviewer asked him to expound on this statement. "For example," the professor said, "if a buttered piece of toast falls on the floor, buttered side down, many people might say, Sod's Law. However, the toast usually falls buttered side down because of the height of the table. Most tables are approximately the same height and the height allows the toast to rotate once on its way down so that it naturally falls on the buttered side down. Cause and effect."

The interviewer persisted, "Surely there are certain types of people who have a propensity for Sod's Law."

"No, I don't see it that way. It is simply how people transfer their beliefs to life."

This conversation reverberated in my head for days. The connection to the principles of Mind, Consciousness and Thought is clear. Cause and effect. As we think, so we are.

It is a marvel to me how this understanding blossoms and opens the mind to seeing nuggets of wisdom woven into the commonplace areas of life. A colleague mentioned that he had just read a business book and found joy in the reading. "Usually I read the latest material available to keep up with the current information in the marketplace and I find it interesting but not joyous. But as I read this material I found many areas where I could see the principles at work and I found that fascinating and joyful.

"The book talked about going beyond the current technology into the unknown and making decisions based on non-quantitive qualities. The book also talked about how people have the capacity for insight. I pondered these statements and could see manifestations of Mind in the creative intelligence of going beyond the known into the unknown. I saw Consciousness acting as an agent for bringing this awareness to light and Thought as the vehicle for conveying this process.

"I'm seeing how you can talk about the principles in business. Often I have bumped into various levels of receptivity and thought I could only talk about the impact the principles have had on my personal life. Now I am seeing the universality of the principles in the marketplace and how to bridge the gap by using common information and connecting this to the principles. Going into the unknown and gaining insight and creativity is certainly principle-based."

Another colleague shared the changes in her role as a traditional team builder in organizations. "As I've learned more about how the principles create experience I find my work changing. I can no longer do my programs in the same way. The technique-based programs that I was trained in don't have the lasting impact I've observed with the principle-based programs I've become familiar with. Now in my classes I find myself talking more about the power of thought in creating our experience and the impact this has on our interpersonal skills.

"We had an interesting experience the other day in a course on group dynamics that I'm taking at university. The instructor told us this was going to be a classroom lab setting to learn interpersonal skills. We were left to our own devices with no instructions on what to do with our time. This experiment took place over two weekends.

"As time progressed, people got frustrated and anxious, and began to make assumptions about each other that created some conflict and angst. I remained calm and curious as I observed and listened. One woman noticed that I wasn't getting upset and asked why. Then more people in the class got curious. I felt a little awkward because I wasn't the facilitator in the session and felt I couldn't say too much. But I did share a little about how helpful thought recognition is and how thought creates feelings. Even the instructor got curious and agreed with me.

"It was obvious to me the difference between techniques and understanding the power of the principles. With this understanding, I was able to maintain my healthy state of mind. I observed that those who were educated in the more traditional techniques didn't have the same response. They appeared uncomfortable with the unknown. When their technique didn't fit the status quo they became disoriented. Yet I found I was curious and interested in the dynamics, felt more certainty in myself and didn't get upset. Frankly, I wasn't really aware of these internal changes until the experiment in group dynamics."

Another colleague shared this story. "A potential client approached me expressing interest in my principle-based work with corporations. His company was experiencing a difficult time with the marketplace; their product was losing the leading edge and they were looking for creative and innovative ways of dealing with this challenge.

"We have some understanding of the role of thought in creating our experience of reality," the client told my friend, "but it's still a struggle to maintain a healthy state of mind during this phase. I try and remember to see the challenge as a thought but it's not easy. Then I feel guilty because I should be able to handle this and change my thinking."

As my friend listened it occurred to him that the client was seeing the role of thought as a concept, as a technique of "change your thinking," rather than seeing the power of principle and the fact that mental health is always available and accessible. Seen from this perspective, there is no struggle to try and maintain a healthy state of mind. The healthy state is already there. It's just a matter of slowing down enough for the health to emerge.

The other thing my friend helped his prospective client to see is that we are the principles in action. There is no methodology to apply or remember. There is just a simple recognition and acceptance of this fact and then observation of the results.

Cause and effect. Think and create. Sod's Law. Murphy's Law. It's how we transfer our beliefs to life. Where do *you* want to live? We have an infinite number of choices.

The Joy of Giving

Preparing for the Christmas season gives me great joy. Every gift wrapped, every decoration put around our home, the menu planned for Christmas Day, all give me pleasure. It doesn't matter whether people appreciate the gift, decorations or food because I feel as if I have already received the feeling of appreciation in the moment or thought of the gift, decoration or menu.

Recently someone commented to me how hurt she was when a gift she had given to someone had not been acknowledged. "I'll not give them another gift. If they can't say thanks then I can't be bothered to send them any more presents. How rude they are not to acknowledge the gift. In my day we always sent a 'bread & butter' note to thank people for their parcel."

This comment brought to mind how I used to feel this way all the time and frankly, depending on my state of mind, how I still can feel this way occasionally. But since I've experienced another way of simply enjoying the giving without thought of receiving thanks, I find it gratifying and refreshing and am open to learning more about giving without expecting anything back.

For example, it occurred to me how freeing it would be to have conversations without expecting connection or understanding. Most conversations are used to connect and understand each other but there are times when it seems like there is not a meeting of the minds, no alignment.

Imagine the freedom of being able to have a conversation with someone without agreeing with each other and having the ability to not take it personally. Imagine having the freedom to not understand each other's point of view and not taking it personally. Imagine being able to give of yourself in a conversation this way, without expecting anything in return. Imagine the freedom and respect that would be maintained if we could operate from that state of mind more of the time.

Giving of ourselves without thought of reciprocal action is a spiritual gift, one that we all have access to and spontaneously experience from time to time. Learning to cultivate and nurture this gift is rich in purpose. There is a sense of fulfillment in pursuing this action, not with intellectual desire but more with an inner knowing that this is possible.

The years that I worked in the inner city brought much understanding of giving without need for reciprocity. I saw that people had so few material possessions that anything I could do to help was little enough. However, the giving of myself had certain conditions, though I didn't realize it at the time. People who didn't have much weren't expected to express appreciation for whatever I gave, whether in my time or gifts of food and clothing. I felt they didn't know any better so I excused them.

However, family and friends were another story. They knew better! Therefore they were expected to express their appreciation and gratitude. The stronger I felt this, the less appreciation I received. It took an insight to move me past this belief. The insight was simply the knowledge that *giving is receiving*. That insight changed my life from one of expectation to one of acceptance.

There was an occasion when we held a program in skid row. At the beginning of the program, our group decided to ask the people what they were grateful for. At first I was stunned that our trainees would ask this question of this particular group of people who were homeless, recovering addicts. I felt it was disrespectful to pose that question. To my complete surprise the question brought forth an overwhelming response of gratitude. People were grateful for a cardboard box for their home, grateful to be in recovery, grateful to have some food on the table and a warm shelter that day. Their response brought tears to my eyes as well as to many others.

Another time, a colleague and I were doing a retreat for people suffering with AIDS. At one point our conversation centered around gratitude and once again, as people found something to be grateful for, the feeling in the room deepened and everyone felt connected. This feeling allowed equality to take place. There was no division between those who had AIDS and those who did not. There was a connection of spirit between human beings. I observed that spirit is the great equalizer.

Experiencing this sense of equality with all people is something I continue to learn. Occasionally it seems more difficult with those I am closest to. There seems to be higher expectations with those you love. It never fails to amaze me that we can be more understanding of others than we can of ourselves or our loved ones. What supports me in this quest of seeing equality is the understanding that this is a lifelong journey and my hope is to travel and enjoy it, bumps and all.

The Resilience of Hope

Recently, I had the good fortune to be invited to visit two agencies providing services to those in need. One agency offers a maternity program for single mothers. This comprehensive program offers a safe haven for women who have no other place to go and also supplies education so they can find work and provide for themselves and their child. The program makes a home and daycare available after the child is born while the mothers continue to work and until the women feel able to go on their own. Usually the women are feeling hopeful, confident and revitalized after the birth and with completing their education most feel that they are ready to leave before their time is up.

The other program is housed in a beautiful old mansion that has been renovated as a halfway home for women who are struggling with substance-abuse addictions. This program is the last step before prison. If they succeed here then after a period of time they are free to continue their lives, free of their addictions and crimes committed to support their habits.

One of the things I noticed was the gentleness underlying the services. There was no patronizing attitude from the staff, no blame, shame or judgment. For the most part there was a respectful and healthy acceptance of the women, no matter what they had done prior to their participation in the program. All the staff and residents in these programs are being trained in the three principles approach.

The trainers who are providing the three principles program are quite remarkable in their understanding. They are gentle and wise and offer much hope to the residents and staff of these agencies. The trainers' understanding of innate health residing in each and every person, no matter the behavior, paves the way for acceptance of what they offer in the principles educational process. The residents and staff quickly resonate with the common sense and logic of the principles and the hopefulness within the individuals is activated within a short time.

Even when there is some resistance, the trainers are wise enough not to confront the resistance but simply keep the feeling level of their interaction healthy. They don't dwell on the details of the resistance and interestingly enough, the resistance is usually defused by the warm and caring feeling. Then the wisdom emerges for those who were confused and therefore resistant.

There is a kindness about this approach that pervades the agencies. As soon as you walk in the front door, you can feel the peace. As I talked with the women in both places, what came clear is that they felt safe and accepted. Yes, there are rules and policies to follow. But the women are so grateful for the safety and health of their environment that they accept the system. At the same time, some of the policies are being reviewed to find better ways to provide the service.

In the maternity program, several of the women I talked with had just arrived a day or two before my visit. They were exhausted and a couple even fell asleep while the rest of us were chatting. The staff accepted and understood their need

for rest and knew that for many of the residents this was prob-
ably the first place they had felt safe enough to rest in quite
some time. One staff member noticed a young woman rub-
bing her forehead and being very quiet. She went over and
whispered to her, "Go and have a sleep and then we'll see you
at dinner." The resident looked grateful and apologized for
not participating, saying she had a migraine. The other young
women noticeably relaxed at the staff's gentle behavior and
opened up even more in their participation.

As our discussion continued, one of the young women
mentioned that she was pursuing her bachelor's degree and
that when her child was born, she would carry on with her
education and have her degree by the time the maternity program was finished. She was grateful for the opportunity and
hopeful for the future. She had a sense of pride in what she
was doing and attributed it to her new understanding of
innate health.

One of the staff told me that when the women first arrive,
they feel hopeless and feel that they are failures. The staff help
them see that taking the step to show up for the program
shows courage, not failure. This idea of courage is a new concept for them. Soon there is a sense of hopefulness, once the
women have time to rest and regroup.

Staff pointed out that what often occurs with the coming
birth of their child, is that many of the women feel a rebirth
within themselves, finding this an opportunity to take stock
of their life and seeing that they have more potential than they
thought they had. The three principles training encourages
this hope, helping the residents and staff see that they always
had this potential within them and that they'll never lose it.

Many of the women spoke of gratitude as a new feeling to experience within themselves. One woman mentioned that she used to be grateful to her boyfriend but when he left her after finding out that she was pregnant, she lost her feeling of gratitude. "I've learned that gratitude comes from within me, that it is a spontaneous feeling of health. I had never felt grateful to myself because I always felt unworthy. Now I feel stronger and more hopeful because I know I have innate health inside myself. For the first time, I feel I can make a life for myself and my baby."

Another resident at the treatment facility talked about a "gratitude assignment" that had been particularly helpful. She said she had nothing to be grateful for until she ended up at this beautiful halfway home. "At first when we were required to think of something to be grateful for, I couldn't come up with anything. I just felt lost and alone and missed the drugs. But now that I'm in recovery and learning about my inner health, I find much to be grateful for.

"Being off drugs and feeling human again has made me grateful. Working in the garden has given me great pleasure and I'm grateful for that. Having the staff and other residents care for me without judgment has helped me so much. Learning to care for myself is a new experience for me. Now I don't need an assignment to find gratitude. I feel grateful just for being alive."

Challenges at Work:
Crisis or Opportunity?

Life is a series of events. Some events are wonderful, joyful and inspiring. Some are ordinary, everyday occurrences. Other situations challenge and test our mettle. Losing one's job is considered one of the most stressful events, whether as a result of downsizing, poor performance or a square peg trying to fit into a round hole.

The separation is challenging not only for the person who is leaving but also for the individual who has the job of informing. One of the questions many people ask, once they have gone through the principles training, is how to handle a situation like this.

Managers are often reluctant to perform this task, seeing it as hurtful to the employee, personally, professionally and financially. The manager thinks that because he is now operating from a healthier perspective he should be able to do more to save that person's job, by coaching, skill upgrading or other creative endeavors. Often this works out very well and both manager and employee rise to the occasion and performance improves.

But occasionally a manager will confide that he feels it is his fault because he couldn't see a way to help his employee, and he perceives he was unsuccessful in his coaching. Sometimes this situation can go on for a long time before the manager comes to grips with the situation and, if necessary, carries out the task of separation. Even with an understanding of the principles, this can be a period of stress and angst, both for the manager and the employee. Seldom is the employee not aware that something is up and often would just prefer to get it over with.

Not only does this situation create unease between manager and employee but it also provides the opportunity for much unrest among the other employees and managers. Morale is quickly affected by this situation as people begin to wonder if they have something to worry about.

Amidst the thinking that permeates these events is how people perceive the three principles and wisdom. Erroneously people conclude that when you begin to access your wisdom, life from then on is lived with grace and ease, with never a stressful moment to be had, forgetting that life is a contact sport and that we will continue to experience stress occasionally.

From this unrealistic thinking, people sometimes feel that if they are stressed, there is something wrong, that they are not "living" from their wisdom. In a perfect world, that is true. But we are not living in a perfect world and to expect the world to be perfect is asking for trouble. Far better to accept what is, change what can be changed, and be grateful for perspective.

It can take a while for people to realize the nature of thought and the relationship between thought and stress. When this realization occurs it defuses stress. So instead of feeling guilty about feeling stressed, we feel grateful for understanding, which allows us to move forward with a fresh perspective and more knowledge.

There is also a pervasive feeling that from wisdom one will be able to find a solution. The interesting thing about this factor is that this is true. *However, the solution may come in a different form than one expects.* Sometimes the solution is so unexpected that it can seem to be invisible. This is where it is helpful to see whether what looks like a crisis is in fact an opportunity.

For example, an attorney friend of mine was unhappy in his position. He vacillated for some time, considered leaving the firm for another company or perhaps even leaving law and pursuing another career. He was reluctant to make a decision to leave and couldn't find it in his heart to see how he could stay. Finally, after a period of months, the decision was taken out of his hands and he was given notice. His boss told him that he could see he was unhappy and had given him numerous opportunities to do other things in the firm, to no avail. So the boss felt there was no other option.

At first my friend struggled with this turn of events, feeling lost and bereft. He said the only thing that helped him was knowing that somehow he was creating this situation and so he didn't feel totally out of control. He went through a period of self-examination and came to the conclusion that it was the best thing that could have happened. The notice to leave had prompted some deep reflection on his part.

He used the time off to learn more about how we create our experiences in life and, in the process, his personal thinking lessened and more calmness and insights occurred. Opportunities began to come his way to travel and to use his knowledge of law in different capacities than he had imagined. He's happy in this new role and trusting that more opportunities will appear. He told me that his feeling of service to mankind is now more important than his attention to fees. Interestingly, he is finding more work at healthier fees than he was earning before.

Another attorney told me her story. She is a partner in a prestigious law firm specializing in corporate law. For a decade she was quite content in her position then became increasingly dissatisfied. She felt that perhaps she might leave the practice of law. She pondered over this for some time as she continued her work. She attended a principles training and found new insight into what she wanted to do. She found new enthusiasm and satisfaction in mediation, part of the judicial system, but a very different function from corporate law. She put out some inquiries in that direction and is delighted to find new opportunities and purpose in her work.

Another example tells of a company purchased by a larger organization. There was duplication of positions so some separation occurred for long-term employees of the smaller company. The employees of the smaller company had several years of principles training. They were understandably concerned about their positions and whether or not they would still have jobs. The larger company retained a number of the employees but many were let go.

Some of the employees told us that they had struggled with what they would do and that had it not been for their understanding of how stress can be increased through their thinking about the situation, they would have felt much worse. Most were able to maintain a fair degree of stability while they looked for other work. In some cases, people were without work for up to a year, yet even these people stated that their understanding of the principles was a godsend to them, helping them weather this time of uncertainty.

Crisis or opportunity? Our choice is in how we look at it.

Both Sides of the Coin

Sometimes it can be difficult to see both sides of the coin. We have all been in situations where we get upset, judgmental, take things personally and see only our perspective. Is there a way to move through this mire of judgment, be it self-assessment or judgment of others? Most times if asked this question I would answer, "Yes." But there are times when the process eludes me. Then I know it is time to slow down and let life unfold. In the unfolding I have discovered that love and patience is the prerequisite to finding the secret of acceptance and seeing both sides of the coin.

Being patient, with yourself and others, provides fertile ground. It may feel dormant at first, as if you're doing nothing. But give it some sunshine and a little fertilizer and understanding grows. Knowing that we are the principles in action helps cultivate the soil. The spiritual principles that we are gifted with, give us the power to create our world, and are always in motion. We are spiritual energy manifested into physical form. Spiritual energy flows through us and is in everything around us.

How easy it is to use this energy, with our free will, to create a world of judgment. How uncomfortable that judgment feels. Much as we try to rationalize judgment, if it feels uncomfortable then we know we are using this spiritual power against ourselves. Still, the game of life is to continually find deeper levels of understanding and to build a world where understanding and love and caring is primary.

Love brings acceptance, allowing us to see both sides of the coin without taking things personally. Acceptance allows us to see what is and what isn't. For example, Susan, a friend of mine, has been struggling with family problems. Susan's daughter, Beth, is experiencing great angst because of a divorce she and her husband have gone through. Beth is feeling hurt, angry, betrayed and bitter about her ex-husband.

Susan has been patient with Beth, listening to her woes and offering comfort to her. But the daughter's lamenting doesn't stop. Susan is soon contributing motherly advice, putting in a word here and a word there, pointing to innocence in both the daughter and the daughter's ex-spouse, seeing both sides of the relationship, both sides of the coin. To Susan's surprise, Beth is infuriated at this and does not want to hear about anyone's innocence, least of all, the man she feels has betrayed her.

This goes on for several conversations until finally Susan sees that Beth wants to be left with her anger and understands that is her prerogative. Susan accepts her daughter's choice even though she doesn't agree with her anger and feels badly because her daughter is suffering from the angry feelings she has. Patience beckons from the love of mother for daughter.

The next time they talk, Susan and Beth agree to move on to other topics. Beth explains that, right now, she just can't bear to hear of either her or her ex-husband's innocence. She tells her mother that she appreciates her help but she needs to find her own way. They have a brief but honest conversation sharing some of their private thoughts. Advice and expectations take a back seat and their relationship grows stronger based on patience and acceptance with love as the catalyst.

In a similar theme, a colleague relates this story: "I have a client I've been coaching. He came to me because he was troubled by his inability to find work. His attitude was pessimistic; he could not see any way that he could get out of his current difficulties. He was fearful of losing his marriage, his home and all that he held dear. Held prisoner by his thoughts of failure and loss, he was immobilized, unable to act.

"As I listened to him I was struck by his ability to articulate his problems clearly and honestly. I found him to be a humble and honest person, so caught up in his thinking that he could no longer see anything worthwhile in himself. When I shared my observations with him, he said, 'I don't feel humble. I feel humiliated.' My response was, 'Humility is the other side of the coin.' This statement left both my client and me thoughtful. Those words had just popped out of my mouth and I wondered where they came from. I knew they were true.

"We spent some time focusing on his strengths, spiritually, personally and professionally, and his thinking cleared up as if by magic. Then as we talked about what career positions were available to him, he fell back into his pessimistic 'that isn't possible, this won't work, that won't work' thinking. After that, almost in the next breath, he mentioned other options he might consider. His mood shifted upward as he regarded both sides of the coin and chose to move toward what *is* possible rather than what *isn't* possible. It was very interesting seeing how quickly his mood shifted according to his thinking.

"My client then asked me about the difference between thought in your head and thought that is spoken or written.

He said 'The act of looking for work, not thinking about looking for work, lies in a different sphere of human experience—action not thought. I am confused about when is thought action and when is thought just thought and would appreciate some clarification.'

"I felt this to be a very curious question and it drew an insight from me. What came to mind is that thought **is** action, whether it is spoken, written or silent in your head. It is always in action in everyone, whether we are aware of it or not. Thought is a neutral, spiritual process that has the power to create form. Thought is a creative action—even if silent in our head, there is still activity. Therefore, if we are thinking 'it isn't possible' thoughts, then it isn't possible and that is the world we create. If we start to consider 'it is possible' then it opens the door to all sorts of possibilities.

"I learned a great deal from my client and I'm glad to say that he has found himself a very good position, and he and his wife are currently in couples counseling."

The story my colleague shared with me left me feeling reflective and I appreciated his words of wisdom. It gave me a fresh perspective on seeing that people have their own path and their own way to learn and grow.

Just as in the first example of Susan and her daughter Beth, there are times when I see a loved one, a dear friend or a colleague making what I perceive to be a mistake and my instinct is to help them. Oftentimes this gets me involved in ways that aren't healthy, either for me or for them. So I continue to learn: *Love–Patience–Acceptance,* and trust that ultimately all paths will converge. There is much to ponder, seeing both sides of the coin.

Is Well-Being Sustainable?

The question, "Is well-being sustainable?" often comes up for people as they experience a shift in understanding and gain new perspective accompanied by positive feelings of well-being. The issue is frequently clouded by assumptions that sustainability means maintaining the peak level of well-being rather than maintaining a shift in level of understanding.

Consider the following for a moment. When an insight is experienced, resulting in a better understanding of life, that is a permanent shift in consciousness. Even though we may experience various levels of thinking and being after that insight, we still have had a permanent shift in understanding. One never goes back to less understanding. We will visit less pleasant feelings from time to time, as all humans do, but we will always have the new level of understanding as a foundation.

An analogy would be in learning how to do math, how to add, subtract, divide, multiply and so on. Once you learn these fundamental principles, you never lose the ability to do math. You never forget that two plus two equals four. No matter that you may be in a bad mood and perhaps find a mathematical problem difficult, you will still know that two plus two equals four, you will still know the principle of addition.

Realizing the fact that a shift in consciousness is sustainable, even when we experience lower moods, brings great relief and acceptance of one's humanness. It also brings more feelings of well-being because there is less judgment, less personal thinking about how we should do better because we know better and so forth.

What a gift to realize that in accepting all the feelings we get, even the unpleasant feelings, we are learning more about how to use the principles more productively. We are learning to view feelings more as information than as an unchanging, permanent state. We are learning to see feelings with more neutrality as we gain the understanding that our thinking creates feelings. Given that knowledge, it makes sense that the more we regret the absence of the initial peak feeling after insight, the more it is that thought gets in the way of new feelings emerging.

It is also helpful to examine whether the goal of life is to maintain that peak feeling of elation or to enjoy the journey? Does the idea that life is about maintaining peak feelings produce a misleading expectation? Does that idea prevent new and original feelings from emerging? Does that idea prevent calmer, gentler, deeper feelings from being experienced and perhaps maintained for longer periods of time rather than just experiencing the flash of powerful energy? Good questions to consider.

Another point to consider is the role of appreciation in helping to maintain well-being. So often we appreciate the peak feeling momentarily then subtly start to regret when the feeling has diminished. What might happen if we appreciated life in all its various colors? If we lived in the feeling of gratitude more of the time, even for the simple joy of finding a parking place closer to our destination, would that make a difference in the quality of well-being? If we took a moment to thank someone close to us for always being there, would that help maintain well-being? Would it enhance our life if we took a moment to smile at a stranger? Might that not also enhance the stranger's life?

At a leadership seminar recently, the group took some time toward the end of the session to express appreciation for what they had learned in the program and what they had learned from each other. The tone of the session shifted to a much warmer feeling of camaraderie and people were obviously touched. Someone commented on how powerful it would be to do this assignment more of the time in their everyday workplace.

Appreciation isn't about an assignment or technique that reminds us to be grateful but sometimes it may start the ball rolling. We have all experienced those moments when the feeling of gratitude spontaneously washes over us without conscious thought, a natural outcome of being at peace, that all is right with the world.

What about appreciating the simple knowledge that we know there is such a thing as spiritual principles that create the human experience? Do we take a moment or two to appreciate the profundity of that knowledge? When we look around the world today with all the unrest and lack of understanding, are we grateful for knowing that deep within us is the strength to travel through the unrest of the world with equanimity? Are we grateful that we have a safe harbor of wisdom within us? What a refreshing and relieving thought.

One man who lives in such a manner told me this story. His friends were noticing that he had changed from a party animal to a gentler, fun-loving person who found great enjoyment in the living of life, seeing all the nuances life has to offer with interest and curiosity. "You are so relaxed and calm," they told him. "It is very disturbing."

Perhaps if we "disturbed" the world more in this manner, the world would be a more restful place. Certainly, our personal world would be more restful and that would help others.

Seeing the Innocence and Seeing the Truth

Seeing the psychological innocence in people is a wonderful, helpful and freeing concept. The term "seeing innocence" is based on the understanding that everyone does the best they can given their thinking at any moment in time. This understanding liberates one from judgment and brings compassion for oneself and for others. It also enhances the ability of people to be accountable for their actions, in a fair and appropriate manner.

Sometimes people think that seeing the psychological innocence in someone means ignoring the situation. Sometimes individuals may blame themselves for "being in their ego" when they see something amiss in a situation or relationship. They don't trust themselves because they feel it's their ego thinking. Often they will attribute what they are seeing solely to the way they are thinking about the situation, ignoring the very real evidence that there may be more going on than meets the eye.

Does the above paragraph sound familiar? Does it hit home? Have you ever had someone who has an understanding of the three principles tell you that "it is just your thinking?" Have you ever doubted what you are seeing because you are feeling judgmental? Have you ever berated yourself because you shouldn't be thinking this way? Have you discovered that when you calm down and your vision clears, the same situation *feels* and *looks* different?

If any of these questions provoke some consideration on your part, then exploration and contemplation may be in order. You may want to consider the principle of Consciousness in allowing you to see beyond ego, *even when ego is present*. Just because ego is present doesn't mean that Consciousness doesn't work. At that point Consciousness is the gift that tells us to look deeper for the answer. Consciousness is the "itch" that you feel the need to scratch. Consciousness is wisdom saying there is more to this picture, and even though ego may be painting a different picture, the itch doesn't go away. That's when you know that wisdom is on standby and will keep tickling you until you look deeper.

You may be seeing something in yourself that isn't serving you well, regarding a judgmental feeling, or feeling bad because you *should* know better. Using the *should* word is always good for some stress mileage, but once you get past the *feeling bad* part, there may be something that others are promoting in the situation that warrants addressing. Just because you feel you are in your ego does not negate the fact that there may be something that others are contributing to the situation that requires exploration, beyond your ego and beyond their egos.

For example, John had been having a tough time with his boss and his work life for quite some time. He felt like nothing he did was satisfactory to his supervisor, who seemed to criticize everything John did to the point that John was ready to call it quits.

What was so surprising about this was that John's boss had been his mentor since he was hired two years before and they had always had a wonderful relationship. Often they would lunch together and discuss various projects and occasionally have a beer after work. So when the relationship gradually changed and the boss seemed to be always on his case, John was puzzled by this turn of events. He wasn't sure how to handle this and was nervous about approaching his supervisor because the roles of mentor and mentored were solidly in place.

John had many sleepless nights and felt bad that what had promised to be a long-term relationship seemed to be dissolving in front of his eyes. Not only that but he was afraid that his job was no longer secure. He had great respect for what he had learned from his mentor and resolved to try to re-establish rapport with him. Yet nothing seemed to work.

John kept mulling over in his mind, "I know it's how I'm thinking about this situation but it seems to me that my boss delights in criticizing my work. Even when others have applauded my projects, my boss voices some concern. What am I doing wrong? It must be me. It must be my ego that doesn't like to be criticized."

John continued to work the best he could with his boss, understanding that his thinking about the situation was a key factor in how he felt. Some of the time he was able to be in a healthy state of mind and the consistent digs and criticism he got from his boss didn't faze him. At other times, when he was feeling less calm, his boss's behavior bothered him. Still he persevered, thinking, "It's me. I'm just into my ego. I know he's innocent of what he's doing because he doesn't know any better. But he's sure ticking me off."

After some contemplation John decided to ask for one more meeting to see if he couldn't work more effectively and harmoniously with his supervisor. He knew that the best way to approach this meeting was to be in a healthy state, calm and curious.

What he realized in this meeting was that his mentor wasn't interested in seeing John get ahead in his career. His mentor felt threatened by John's creativity, by his ability to draw the best out of the rest of the team and by his calm demeanor. Once John realized this it was like a weight off his shoulders. He felt such relief to realize that his mentor was human too! Like the rest of us, John's boss had his own insecurities that played out in his reluctance to see his protégé move ahead, perhaps thinking his own job might be in question.

With the clarity that came to John, he was able to reassure his mentor, without words, but simply by being aware of and more in service to help his boss feel safe. John knew that whatever the outcome, he was in a much better position to handle it because of this new understanding. Seeing the innocence and seeing the truth serves us all well. One does not negate the other.

Conceptual Models:
Help or Hindrance?

Professionals using the three principles approach in their work often look for ways to better articulate the principles of Mind, Consciousness and Thought. This articulation is done with the best intentions to be of service to their clients and to help people understand the logic of the principles. A case in point: a practitioner will have an insight and from that insight develop a model to explain what they realized. In that moment of time the model does an excellent job of illustrating the point. However, the problem comes when the model becomes the point rather than the insight. Then the model can be a dis-service to the clients.

Because of the nature of Thought and the fact that Thought flows and changes from moment to moment, the model may no longer be relevant. There may be a simpler way of explaining the point you are trying to make. In addition, if you stick to the model that has been developed, you can be prevented from learning anything new. The model becomes static, whereas wisdom is fluid.

A common term that is used in the transfer of knowledge is "transfer of competency." That same term is sometimes applied to the sharing of wisdom. Perhaps there might be a more representative term when the sharing of wisdom is con-cerned. Transfer of competency infers that the one to whom competency is being transferred does not have competency to begin with. If we are looking at the understanding surrounding the three principles, a basic premise is that we all have innate mental health. So does the transfer of competency mean people don't have innate health?

Perhaps the transfer of competency is more the transfer of the "form" of competency. And that is where models come into play. People feel that in order to teach others how to become better leaders, clinicians, educators or whatever, form is needed. And to a degree that is true. We all know that education is based on the written word. What the understanding of the principles brings to the table is the partnership of form and formless, of intellect and wisdom.

Consider this: The whole purpose of sharing the knowledge of the principles with others is to act as a catalyst to their wisdom awakening. From that point on, the engine is running and wisdom is unfolding within that individual at his or her own pace. Certainly there is benefit in continuing to fan the flame or stoke the engine but there is a point when that can get in the way of the engine operating at its full capacity.

There was a time, in the principles understanding, when the "thought cycle" was representative of how thought worked. The model was this: thought creates feeling, which creates behavior leading to a result. We would draw a circle with thought at the top, then going clockwise a quarter way around was feeling, then at the bottom was behavior, then continuing around the circle was results, then back to thought.

We used this model to show that if you changed the thought then the feeling would change, consequently the behavior and results of that behavior. It was a wonderful and

practical tool. Many practitioners who had the three principles as their foundation used this model to illustrate the role
of thought.

I also valued and counted on this model. I used the model
so extensively that it became the basis of my work and the
three principles were in the background. Quite a few years
ago, at a principles conference, one of the themes was to move
away from the thought model, to trust that new and original
wisdom would come forth in the moment to explain the role
of thought rather than continuing to depend on the thought
cycle.

Indignation rose in me at this suggestion; I felt that if I
let the thought cycle go I would have nothing as practical
and helpful to count on for my trainings. This would be
especially true in disadvantaged communities where practical, down-to-earth presentations are a must. I confronted
one of the presenters at the conference and demanded an
explanation, declaring how valuable this model was for my
work and how much people got from it.

The presenter didn't take umbrage at my tone or stance
but rather listened respectfully and intently to what I had to
say. Then she explained, "What we're seeing is that many people are believing the thought cycle to be the same as the positive thought approach that is so prevalent and it is confusing
to people. Then people think that they have to change their
thoughts by will power and this adds stress to their already
stressful lives. The point we're making is that people change
via insight. When your thinking expands because you realize
something new, then your feelings and behavior automatically
change.

"Also we are seeing that the model is getting in the way of people accessing even more wisdom because as long as you have the model in front of you, and you come to depend on it, it becomes a barrier to any new wisdom emerging."

The explanation made perfect sense to me and I thanked the instructor for her patience in taking the time with me. I realized in that moment that I had become a prisoner of the thought model. My presentations had lost their vitality and I hadn't realized why. I was getting bored with the repetition and, of course, so was my audience.

The next training I gave, my insecurity was reawakened and once more I brought out my old standby model. However this time, the words were dead weight and I no sooner started my old spiel than something stopped me and I flipped over the paper on the flip chart where I had drawn my circle with the thought cycle, and said to the audience, "Bear with me, but this doesn't adequately express what I want to say. Let me explain this in another way."

What came out of my mouth was new, fresh and vital and had impact on the audience and on me. I never went back to that model again. I have nothing against it and see that it has a practical value but I always explain the principles to the best of my ability, in the moment, with whatever comes to mind and whatever is relevant to the audience. I count on and depend on wisdom to come through in a fresh and original way.

Another example of a model that can get in the way of original thought is a concept known as "range of capacities of the mind." This model was developed around 1997 when I was working with Dr. Roger Mills, one of the leading psychologists in this understanding. The intent of the model was to demonstrate that there are many ways of using the power of Mind. With this in mind we identified seven capacities that the mind is capable of:

Wisdom–Insight–Common Sense–Perspective–Analysis–Processing–Memory.

We showed one graphic where all seven capacities are available in a healthy state of mind and pointed out this is the way the mind is designed to work. Then we showed another graphic where the words *Wisdom–Insight–Common Sense–Perspective* were covered slightly with gray. We grayed these words out to illustrate that when we use the intellect to analyze without wisdom we are relying solely on memory and personal thinking.

The purpose of the illustration was simply to show that the most productive way to live was in a healthy state of mind, where all capacities function in the most natural, beneficial way. When we're functioning from a less healthy state of mind, we have less wisdom, insight, common sense and perspective.

This model made perfect sense at the time and I remember that Roger and I were elated to have come up with something that was beneficial to us and we felt would be beneficial to others. "Range of capacities" continued to serve us and many other practitioners very well for several years. I've had countless people tell me how helpful this model has been in deepening their understanding.

There came a point when I saw this concept getting in the way of people discovering their own way of articulating what they were learning. Instead, they would go to the "range of capacities" model and repeat what they had learned by rote. There was a lack of originality in the presentation.

Equally concerning was that people assumed there were only seven capacities to which humans had access and that there were seven ways to use thought. Again that was an erroneous conclusion. In reality everything is Thought and humans have limitless capacities. We had never meant for the "range" to be so limiting. I began to wish that we had never come up with that model and when I heard someone repeating it without their own slant on it, I would take the time to gently probe and see why that point was important to them.

What was so rewarding to me was that when people took a moment to consider my question they would always come up with their own answers in a powerful, meaningful way. It often surprised them and inevitably showed them that they knew more than they thought they did. It also clearly demonstrated the power of *their* wisdom. It always touched me when they drew on their wisdom rather than repeating someone else's. And that serves all of us well.

I've had people agree with me on the risk of creating models and then they continue to present and teach their models anyway. Their rationale is that they have new stories to tell to illustrate their point so the model can stay the same. Can it? Or is there something else waiting in the wings? What role does insight play? What is fertile ground for insights to manifest?

Is it an open mind or is it a mind attached to a model?

Be Gentle With Yourself

One of the issues that people struggle with is whether it is necessary to experience stress and negativity in order to learn. We know that insights come with a positive feeling. If that is the case then how do we resolve the fact that sometimes, as we are transitioning to another level of understanding, we experience feelings of unease, unrest and general malaise?

This is an interesting question for you to contemplate. A colleague and I had this discussion as we shared our experiences of a shift in a level of consciousness. My friend had been going through a rather uneasy time. He described it as "a feeling of nervousness and unease about what the future holds." Further, he described the ability to be in the moment when he was in a meeting or with his family and acknowledged that he was finding that he was still very productive. Nonetheless, he was still feeling periods of unrest and anxiety and did not appreciate those feelings. What to make of this situation?

As we explored the power of Thought in creating our feelings, my friend pointed out that he knew about this power but it didn't seem to be working all the time. "Why is that?" I asked. "Because these feelings won't go away," he responded. "Even when I try to stop the negative thinking, it doesn't help."

"Didn't you say that there are times when you are able to be in the moment and at that point the negative thoughts aren't in your head?"

"Yes."

"And didn't you also say that you are more productive now during this transition than you were two years ago when you didn't understand the role of Thought?"

"Yes, that's true. But I still am feeling anxious and uneasy and have been feeling this way about a number of things for some time. I have a big project coming up soon and I'm nervous about how it's going to turn out. I'm not worried about what I'm going to say but I'm nervous about whether I'll have a panic attack before my presentation and then I'll freeze and won't be able to do anything. Four years ago I experienced this intense nervousness before a presentation and I don't want to make the same mistake. I have high expectations of myself and don't want to be a failure."

"Be gentle with yourself," I advised my friend. "You're a different person now than you were four years ago. Those high expectations are ego based and are getting in the way of acceptance, learning and achievement. Allow your wisdom to emerge and you'll be fine and will achieve more that you can imagine."

We continued to explore this situation. As I listened, it seemed to me that my friend was making an issue over something that was a natural preparation, a spiritual preparation for more grounding, more understanding of how the principles of Mind, Consciousness and Thought work in everyday life. It reminded me of times when I'd felt exactly the same, times when I felt a cold ball of insecurity in the pit of my stomach for no real reason.

The more I entertained these thoughts of unease, the more the feelings lingered. I felt irritated that the feelings lasted. Didn't I know better? Then why were the feelings persisting?

It wasn't fair! What was I missing? It finally dawned on me that I was learning some humility and acceptance for what is and not looking for what isn't.

As I shared these thoughts, my friend was silent for a time and then began to talk. "I've just realized that I've been fighting these feelings and running away from them because I thought that we only learned from positive feelings. It just occurred to me that was very limiting. I'm also realizing that I wasn't accepting those feelings of unease with understanding and perspective and that while I was fighting them, I was doing so on a personal level, with ego. This is what has been keeping the feelings alive in my reality rather than understanding and appreciating the role of Thought which turns unease into ease. It's very humbling to see this and I'm feeling so much better now."

My friend pointed out that the Latin word for humility is "humilitas" which means ground. "So humility is grounding," he concluded thoughtfully.

We spent some quiet moments together absorbing this powerful insight then each of us went our own way. What occurred to me later was that the learning did happen via a positive feeling—the positive moment of acceptance, understanding that we all have those times of unease with the unknown future. This healthy acceptance allows wisdom to emerge immediately, bringing with it positive feelings. Acceptance and well-being happens simultaneously.

It also occurred to me that people can get stuck in the struggle and think that the struggle is what creates the learning or releases the creative juices. It's not until the understanding comes that the struggle stops. It is the understanding that brings solutions to the struggle so that the angst ceases.

Many times people have mentioned geniuses, artists, scientists or other gifted individuals who were brilliant in their work but had miserable personal lives. Perhaps they did not understand the role of Thought in creating their world and therefore experienced spontaneous times of creativity but didn't know how to sustain it.

We are blessed, indeed, to know that there are principles underlying the human experience. Knowing there are principles provides a solid, dependable foundation from which to build and live our lives, in all aspects—work, play, quiet time, as geniuses in our own right—in our everyday life. Living a life of harmony ripples out into the world and can touch and change others. Such is our legacy.

Resources

Banks, Sydney. *Second Chance*. Duval-Bibb Publishing Co., 1989

Banks, Sydney. *In Quest of the Pearl*. Duval-Bibb Publishing Co., 1990

Banks, Sydney. *The Missing Link*. International Human Relations Consultants, Inc., 1998

Banks, Sydney. *The Enlightened Gardener*. International Human Relations Consultants, Inc., 2001

Banks, Sydney, *Dear Liza*. Lone Pine Publishing, 2004

Mills, Roger / Spittle, Elsie. *The Wisdom Within*. Lone Pine Publishing, 2001

Mills, Roger / Spittle, Elsie. *The Health Realization Primer – Empowering Individuals and Communities*. Lone Pine Publishing, 2003

Sydney Banks: **www.sydneybanks.org**
Publisher/Distributor: **www.lonepinepublishing.com**
Elsie Spittle: **www.3phd.net**

All titles listed above are distributed by Lone Pine Publishing.

Lone Pine Publishing

10145 - 81 Avenue	1808 B Street NW, Suite 140
Edmonton, AB, Canada	Auburn, Washington, USA
T6E 1W9	98001

Phone: 1-800-661-9017 1-800-518-3541
Fax: 1-800-424-7173   1-800-548-1169

About the Author

Elsie Spittle has been an internationally recognized trainer and consultant for almost three decades. She was among the first to develop training programs for corporations and communities based on the understanding of the Three Principles of Mind, Consciousness and Thought.

You will also enjoy the following Lone Pine book by the same author!

The Wisdom Within
by Dr. Roger Mills and Elsie Spittle

In this groundbreaking book, important discoveries about your natural inner source of resiliency and healthy psychological functioning are revealed. The authors' 20-year-mission to share these findings has resulted in a series of triumphs that took them from the roughest city streets to the most successful corporate boardrooms.

5.25" x 8.25" • 176 pages
Hardcover • $18.95 CDN • $12.95 US
ISBN-13: 978-1-55105-288-5
ISBN-10: 1-55105-288-1

"The discoveries shared in this book reveal the common source of self-esteem, well-being and a deep inner wisdom. A must read for anyone wanting a better, happier life."

— Jack Canfield, co-author of *Chicken Soup for the Soul*™ series